What's Up w the Church Down the Street?

Leader's Guide
by Thea Nyhoff Leunk

FAITH ALIVE®
Christian Resources

Grand Rapids, Michigan

Unless otherwise indicated, Scripture quotations in this publication are
from the HOLY BIBLE, NEW INTERNATIONAL VERSION, © 1973, 1978, 1984,
International Bible Society. Used by permission of Zondervan Bible Publishers.

Faith Alive Christian Resources published by CRC Publications.
What's Up with the Church Down the Street? Church school materials for high
school students. © 2002, CRC Publications, 2850 Kalamazoo Ave. SE, Grand
Rapids, Michigan 49560. All rights reserved. Printed in the United States of
America on recycled paper.

We welcome your comments. Call us at 1-800-333-8300 or e-mail us at
editors@faithaliveresources.org.

ISBN 1-56212-785-3

10 9 8 7 6 5 4 3 2

Acknowledgments

This curriculum is the end of a journey that involved the help of many people. To all of you I say thanks.

- To Joe Coalter, Jim Lewis, and John Mulder of Louisville Presbyterian Seminary, whose course on twentieth-century American Protestantism was the initial spark.

- To Lyle Bierma of Calvin Theological Seminary for guiding the research, sharing family trees, and for always being willing to answer "just one more question."

- To the adult Sunday school class of Glendale Presbyterian Church of Cincinnati, Ohio, for being the first group to let me attempt to teach this material.

- To Crosspoint Christian Reformed Church of Cincinnati, Ohio, for encouraging me to get it into print.

- To editor Bob Rozema for coming out of retirement to apply his gentle pressure and high standards.

For Elissa, Anneke, and Jarrett, my co-authors.

Contents

How to Use This Course

"One holy catholic church" is how we speak of the church of Jesus Christ. Whether we are Baptists, Methodists, or Reformed/Presbyterians, if we confess Jesus as Lord and Savior, we bear the name Christian, and together we are his church. But the truth is, often we don't know what separates us from other Christian traditions or denominations. Ignorance, distrust, lack of respect, and fear can keep us from understanding those differences and appreciating our commonalities.

Goals

This course will help you and your group become acquainted with the various traditions that comprise Christianity as it is seen and experienced in the North American context. As we learn more about the history, theology, and worship practices of these traditions, we hope to replace inaccurate perceptions with a realistic portrait of each faith tradition. We also hope that a solid understanding of others' theology will help us articulate what our own tradition asks of us and enrich our own faith journey. Most of all, we hope it helps us "commit ourselves to seeking and expressing the oneness of all who follow Jesus" (from *Our World Belongs to God: A Contemporary Testimony*, stanza 44).

Organization and Materials

What's Up with the Church Down the Street? is a ten-session course for high school students on the history, theology, and worship practices of ten major traditions in North American Christianity. These are presented from a Reformed, Protestant context, but care has been taken to be truthful and also affirmative and appreciative of fellow Christians in these traditions.

The sessions are designed to inform, explain, and raise key distinctions between these traditions and Reformed thought and practice. By discussing these differences, you and your group will be able to articulate more clearly your own beliefs.

Each session will focus on one of these traditions, which are presented in the chronological or historical order of their founding. The "Christian family tree," which is repeated in each participant newspaper, provides a visual picture of the relationship of each new tradition to the others as the tree grows various branches and limbs.

The course includes ten participant **newspapers**—one for each tradition. Each is organized around common elements. Three major articles focus on the history of the tradition, its theology, and its worship practices. Other articles offer information on unique vocabulary or concepts, writers, key leaders or theologians, the church's governance model, and samples of its confessions, prayers, and writings. These newspapers offer summary portraits of each tradition, not detailed accounts. You'll want to use other reference materials—including websites—for deeper and broader perspectives.

You should not attempt to read the entire newspaper in a one-hour session. This leader's guide will help you select which articles to use in the classroom and which to leave for the students to read at home. Have group members take their newspapers home at the end of every session. You might also suggest that they save the papers for future reference.

The **leader's guide** includes one session for each tradition. It outlines which newspaper articles to read and discuss. It also highlights ways to extend the session both inside and outside the classroom and suggests how to use the materials in an adult setting.

If you are considering also using the course *Which Way to God?* you'll want to teach it before this course, not after it.

Time Frame

The sessions are designed to last an hour. If you have less time than that, you'll need to omit some of the activities we suggest and shorten others. This leader's guide offers suggestions for saving time in every session—please see the end of each "Session at a Glance" section. Look for the **bold type** that suggests how to trim the session to fit your time requirements.

On the other hand, the sessions can easily be expanded. You could add thirty minutes to an existing session to make a single, ninety-minute session, or you could spend two one-hour classes for each tradition. It would be possible, for instance, to begin with one of the videos suggested in this guide, then follow with the discussion of the newspaper. Or to teach a review of the Reformed tradition by spending one session learning about each tradition, and a second on a Reformed response to it. Suggestions for extending the session are included at the end of every session.

You may also want to add two more sessions for field trips to other churches. **We highly recommend, in fact, that you visit at least one other church during the course of this study.** Locate "the church down the street," attend worship there, and meet with its pastor or its youth group. What better way to demonstrate to the class the intent of this course? (If the church down the street happens to be one in the Reformed/Presbyterian tradition, extend your search to another church!)

This course is written and intended for high school students, but you may plan to adapt it for use with adults. If so, be sure to ascertain the interests and backgrounds of your members as you plan the course. For example, if a large number of those in your group are Catholics or ex-Catholics, you may want to plan two sessions on Roman Catholicism so that you have enough time to discuss the differences between that tradition and Reformed practice.

If you are using this course in a day school setting, you can expand it into a quarter of study by combining it with United States or Canadian history, literature, and architecture. Supplement the course with expanded research, biographies, guest speakers, field trips, video resources, and media presentations.

Getting Started

Here is an outline you may want to use for planning this course:

1. Read quickly through the course materials—enough to capture the flavor of the participant newspapers and the overall direction of the course.

2. Decide how many sessions you wish to use. Consider the unique circumstances of your group (past affiliations of the members, the "church down the street," level of interest, local history, possible field trips, and the like) and map these out on a calendar. Check to see if any major Christian holidays fall near any of your scheduled sessions. For instance, you may want to

consider having your group attend an Easter service at an Eastern Orthodox Church or a Christmas midnight mass at a Catholic Church.

3. Decide which field trips you will organize and make initial contacts. Plan the trip for a time *after* your group has discussed the tradition. Consider making two field trips—one to a highly liturgical church such as Eastern Orthodox, Roman Catholic, Episcopal, or Lutheran, and another to the church literally down the street. If these are the same, then consider a second trip to a Baptist or Pentecostal church. (See *Getting Outside the Room*, p. 10, for other field trip ideas.)

4. Research some additional resources for your group. Check the TRAVARCA offerings (see pp. 13-16) to see if you'd like to reserve a video. (Always feel free to substitute a video or part of a video for reading the resource.) Check out resources in your local library in both the adult and juvenile sections, and visit the websites listed in the newspapers. You may also want to purchase some of the print resources listed below; they will be excellent additions to your church library when your course is finished.

5. As time permits, do some extra reading: perhaps a brief history of Christianity to gain a broader perspective of our faith or *A.D.: A Study of Church History* (for young teens; available from Faith Alive Christian Resources). Do some research on the denominational heritage of the church your group will be visiting; review Reformed theology with books like *Quest of Faith* or *Reformed: What It Means, Why It Matters* (also available from Faith Alive Christian Resources).

6. Think about the room your group will be meeting in and decide how you will enhance the space (see *Thinking Inside the Room,* below). Begin your preparations or ask someone to assist you.

7. You may occasionally want to assign various sections of some of the newspapers to members of your group to read at home and present to the group at the next session. For example, one pair of students might be assigned the main history article, another the article on beliefs, and a third the article on worship. Students would read the entire newspaper (as well as their assigned articles) and perhaps investigate other resources such as the suggested websites. They would then meet during the first part of the next session to decide how to present their information in an interesting way to the group.

8. Prepare a calendar for your group and for their parents to be distributed at the first session. You may also wish to purchase folders or notebooks in which your group members can keep the newspapers and other handouts.

Thinking Inside the Room	Use your meeting space to help create interest in the sessions. Here are some ideas to consider; you'll probably have even better ones!

- Go through the participant newspapers and find interesting quotes. Write or print these out on brightly colored paper and post in the room.

- Visit your local library and pick up some books on some or all of the faith traditions. Bring these into the room and display them. Let group members borrow them to read.

- Find biographies of the people featured in the newspapers and make them accessible to the group.

- Make a display of the resources you located in your local library. Picture books from the juvenile section will add color and interest.

- Create a three-dimensional version of the Christian family tree out of paper and have it "grow" across the walls of your room. Or consult an art project book about how to create a freestanding tree that you can construct with simple materials. You could even bring in a real tree or a big branch secured in a bucket of sand.

- If you're studying this during the Christmas season, bring in an artificial Christmas tree and have the group create an ornament for each of the various Christian traditions. If you're studying this during Lent, create symbols for each tradition and hang them on a large section of grapevine.

- If these ideas aren't feasible, take the blank version of the family tree on page 32 to a copy store and have it enlarged to poster size (or do it yourself freehand). Hang it in your room and fill it in as the course progresses.

- Save the church ads from your local paper and display them. As your group studies each denomination, find their local congregations in the ads. Note the names of the churches—do they make more sense having studied the denomination? Survey the group to determine if any of the churches are "down the street" from someone in your group.

- Bring in a map of your area and identify the homes of each participant with pins or tacks in the same color. Have each participant determine which church is closest to his or her home. Take a camera and go with the whole group on a road trip to take pictures of these churches. Develop the pictures, arrange them on the map, and label them. Refer to them as you study that tradition. Ask participants to do some research on their churches: time of worship, size, ministries, and so on, and to be prepared to share it at the appropriate time.

- Create a similar photo display for the church down the street from your own church. Use pictures, literature, worship resources—whatever information you can find.

- Ask to borrow Christian artifacts from others in your congregation and display them. Icons, crucifixes, rosaries, different types of communion wafers, worship resources, banners—whatever you can beg or borrow. A local Christian book and materials store may be willing to lend you some of these items.

Getting Outside the Room	The best way to help your group learn more about these other Christian traditions is to facilitate their firsthand experience. Consider adding the following to the course:

- Invite a leader from another denomination to visit your group and share his or her tradition with you. For example, someone from a highly liturgical Christian tradition could lead your group through its worship service, explaining the purpose and movement of the liturgy. You could extend this by attending such a service.

- Hold a joint meeting with the youth group from "the church down the street." Arrange get-acquainted games, food, and a topic of mutual discussion or a service project.

- Using your denominational hymnal and the music resources of your church (including your music director), locate hymns that are gifts to the Christian faith from other traditions. Sing them to open or close your sessions, or invite your music person to lead a session on the music. Include singing and discussion of the theology of the songs.

- Find recordings of the worship music of these traditions and play them for your group.

- Contact your local historical society to find out if the history of any particular Christian tradition is unique to your area. If a historical site or place of worship has been preserved, arrange a visit with an informed guide. Look in particular for groups or communities that attempted to create colonies or utopian societies.

- Has any particular piece of your own denomination's history been key to the history or settlement of your locality? If so, consider including this as an extension of the course. Contact your judicatory office for help with this, if available.

- If a college or university of one of these traditions is located nearby, arrange a campus tour for your group.

Hosting a Guest from Another Christian Tradition

Making the Arrangements
1. Ask the speaker for some background information you can use to introduce him or her to the group.
2. Arrive at a mutual understanding about expenses and honorarium. Always offer an honorarium and/or reimbursement for travel.
3. Find out if your guest has any special physical needs.
4. Know what kind of equipment is needed.
5. Let the speaker know what to expect about the size and age of the group, its knowledge of the subject matter, the room where he or she will be speaking, and the time available. Be clear about where your guest should enter the church or facility.
6. Follow up your conversation with a letter confirming your agreement and enclose directions and your phone number.
7. Prepare discussion questions in advance of the visit.

The Day of the Visit
1. Make sure all the equipment works, the room is set up with the right number of chairs, and everything is physically ready before your guest arrives.
2. Meet your guest at the door (don't make her look for you), and greet her warmly.
3. Introduce the guest to your group.
4. Make sure there's time for any questions and answers. Be prepared with some yourself—the group may be too shy to start asking questions right away.
5. End on time. Be sure to thank the guest, and have the group do so too. Escort the guest to the door.

After the Visit
Write a thank-you note from yourself and the group within the week. If you haven't already given it, include any honorarium or expense reimbursement in the thank you.

How to Visit Another Christian Church

Before the Visit

1. Call the place of worship ahead of time to let the pastor know of your visit and the reason for it.
2. Find out the time of the service and how long it lasts. If your group is large, ask where they should sit.
3. Find out if there are any clothing guidelines or traditions that should be observed.
4. Ask if there is someone who could meet with your group after the service to answer questions and provide a quick tour of the building.
5. Do what you can to prepare the group to participate in and understand the worship service they will be attending. Read the participant newspaper ahead of time, and describe any aspects of the service that might be unfamiliar to the group. If there are any parts of the service in which the host church would not want visitors to participate, make that clear. If you can, find a copy of *How to Be a Perfect Stranger: A Guide to Etiquette in Other People's Religious Ceremonies,* edited by Stuart M. Matlins and Arthur J. Magida. Use it to help prepare your group for a worship field trip.

The Visit

1. Arrive in good time.
2. Encourage the group to be respectful of the worship space of the host church.

After the Visit

1. Meet together as a group as soon as possible afterward and share your impressions.
2. If special arrangements were made to meet the group, tour the building, and so forth, be sure to send a thank-you note to those involved.

Additional Resources

Print Resources

Handbook of Denominations in the United States by Frank S. Mead.
Includes a brief review of the history and beliefs of each major tradition and lists each denominational group within the tradition. Useful as a quick reference. Look for the most recent edition.

A History of Christianity in the United States and Canada by Mark A. Noll.
Lengthy, definitive study. Use the index to look up particular topics.

How to Be a Perfect Stranger: A Guide to Etiquette in Other People's Religious Ceremonies, edited by Stuart M. Matlins and Arthur J. Magida.
Lets you know what to expect when worshiping with another denomination. Helps prepare your group for a worship field trip.

131 Christians Everyone Should Know, edited by Mark Gallie and Ted Olsen.
Well-written, easily accessible collection of biographies.

Protestants in America by Mark A. Noll.
Part of a series called Religion in American Life written by leading scholars for junior high/senior high students. Other titles in the series that relate to this course: *Religion in Colonial America, Religion in Nineteenth-Century America, Religion in Twentieth-Century America, Catholics in America, Orthodox Christians in America, African-American Religion, Immigration and American Religion, Women and American Religion.* Illustrated.

The Story of Christianity by Michael Collins and Matthew A. Price.
  A global view of the Christian story as opposed to a North American one.
  Full-page photographs and illustrations are the best of any current text
  about Christianity. Published by DK (Dorling Kindersley).

Yearbook of American and Canadian Churches, 2002 edition.
  The standard source for learning about any denomination in North
  America. Published annually, statistics are the most current available. Look
  for it in the reference section at your library.

Video Resources

These resources are available from TRAVARCA, an audiovisual library serving
the Reformed Church in America and the Christian Reformed Church in
North America. For information and updates to the list below, contact
TRAVARCA at 1-800-968-7221 or orders@rca.org.

We thank Jane Schuyler, director of TRAVARCA, for compiling this list. You
may contact Jane with questions about these videos at jschuyler@rca.org or at
the number above.

1. The Orthodox Churches
The History of Orthodox Christianity. Three-part series includes *The
  Beginnings, Byzantium,* and *A Hidden Treasure.*
Russian Orthodox Alaska (Landmarks of Faith series), 46 minutes. Features Saint
  Michael's Russian Orthodox Cathedral of Sitka, Alaska.
Russian Orthodoxy: Russian Rites (Introduction to World Religions series),
  15 minutes. Examines the rituals of the Russian Orthodox Church.

2. The Roman Catholic Church
California Missions (Landmarks of Faith series), 46 minutes. Witness everyday
  life in the missions; see their austere and astonishing beauty as you tour the
  Carmel Mission, Mission San Juan Bautista, and the "Queen of the
  Missions"—the Mission of Santa Barbara.
Catholic Churches of Old New Mexico (Landmarks of Faith series), 45 minutes.
  Documentary includes a look at these churches' influence on religion and
  architecture.
Catholic Maryland (Landmarks of Faith series), 46 minutes. View Elizabeth Ann
  Seton's work with children and the watershed career of Archbishop James
  Gibbons, who led the Catholic Church into mainstream American life.
Entertaining Angels: The Dorothy Day Story, 112 minutes. The story of the
  founder of the Catholic Worker movement.
Listening for God (Vol. 1). Eight-session course includes a 12-minute segment
  on writer Flannery O'Connor.
Mother Teresa, 82 minutes. Definitive portrait.
Pioneers of the Spirit series. Contains 24-minute documentaries on several
  prominent Catholics: *Augustine of Hippo; Dante Alighieri; Hildegard of Bingen;
  Ignatius Loyola; Julian of Norwich;* and *Teresa of Avila.*
Roman Catholicism: Flowers in May (Introduction to World Religions series),
  15 minutes. Tells about the Flores de Mayo Festival and the importance of
  the Virgin Mary to Filipino Catholics and explains the significance of the
  pope and of various rituals connected with the faith, including the mass,
  confession, and Holy Communion.
Romero, 105 minutes. Drama of martyr Archbishop Oscar Romero of
  El Salvador.
The Sunday Mass. Focusing on worship, this series includes *Lift Up Your Hearts:
  The Eucharistic Prayer; Say Amen! To What You Are: The Communion Rite; We
  Shall Go Up With Joy: The Entrance Rite;* and *The Word of the Lord: The Liturgy
  of the Word.*

Taizé: That Little Springtime, 26 minutes. The story of this ecumenical community in France and its founder, Brother Roger.

Trappist, 56 minutes. The reality of a monk's life as it is lived at Mepkin Abbey, a Trappist monastery built in 1993 in South Carolina, combined with startling and beautiful images of the past to explore how a monk fits into our modern world. A fine documentary.

3. The Lutheran Tradition

Bonhoeffer: Agent of Grace, 90 minutes. Drama tells the story of Dietrich Bonhoeffer. Documentary programs include *Bonhoeffer: A Life of Challenge* and *Dietrich Bonhoeffer: Memories and Perspectives.*

The Christian Story. Six-part series features Martin Marty; includes *Listening for God* (Vol. 1). A twelve-minute segment in this eight-session course features Garrison Keillor.

Lutheran Roots in America. The story of German, Swedish, Norwegian and other Lutheran immigrants as they made their way to the new world.

Martin Luther. *Luther Legacy; Martin Luther: The Heretic; Where Luther Walked; Martin Luther: Protestant Reformer; Martin Luther/John Calvin,* and Reformation Overview series. Contact TRAVARCA to make a selection.

Writers Reading with Walter Wangerin and *The Book of God* feature author and storyteller Walter Wangerin.

4. The Presbyterian and Reformed Tradition

Celebration! Who Do We Say We Are?, 23 minutes. Introduces the United Church of Christ.

Celebration of Full Communion Worship, 30 minutes. The Reformed Church in America, Evangelical Church in America, Presbyterian Church (USA), and United Church of Christ celebrate their first full communion under the Formula of Agreement.

Frederick Buechner (Faces on Faith series) and *Listening to God* (Vol. 1) feature interviews with Buechner.

Gathered from Many Nations: The Early Years of the Reformed Church in America, 1628-1776, 15 minutes. A historical overview of the Reformed Church in America.

John Calvin. *My Heart I Offer: The Influence of John Calvin in Today's World; Martin Luther/John Calvin;* and the Reformation Overview series highlight Calvin's life.

John Knox, 50 minutes. Re-creates the life and work of Scotland's greatest reformer. Shot on location in Geneva and Scotland.

Kathleen Norris. *Discovering Everyday Spirituality* (parts 3-4), *Kathleen Norris* (Faces on Faith series), and *Listening for God* (Vol. 2) feature interviews with Norris.

Lewis Smedes. *Wrestling with Angels* (episode 4) features Smedes.

Liturgy and Life: A Reformed Understanding of Worship, 26 minutes. Background information and theological reflection on the important elements of Reformed worship. A companion video, *The Meaning of Mystery: Baptism and Communion,* introduces the Reformed understanding of the sacraments.

Martin Luther. *Luther Legacy; Martin Luther: The Heretic; Where Luther Walked; Martin Luther: Protestant Reformer; Martin Luther/John Calvin;* and Reformation Overview series. Contact TRAVARCA to make a selection.

Our Family Album: The Unfinished Story of the Christian Reformed Church, 110 minutes. Dramatic introduction to the Christian Reformed Church.

The Presbyterians and Princeton (Landmarks of Faith series), 46 minutes. Explores the Presbyterian influence on American education.

Robert Schuller (Faces on the Faith series) contains an interview with Schuller.

Who Are We Presbyterians, 17 minutes. Describes what it means to be Presbyterian.

5. The Episcopal/Anglican Tradition

Christ Church: Philadelphia (Landmarks of Faith series), 48 minutes. Built to establish the authority of the Church of England, by 1776 Christ Church had already become dedicated to the ideas of democracy and religious freedom.

C. S. Lewis Through the Shadowlands, 73 minutes. Drama focuses on Lewis's marriage to Joy Davidman.

Madeleine L'Engle. *Writers Reading with Madeleine L'Engle* and *Wrestling with Angels* (episode 5) feature L'Engle.

6. Radicals and Reformers

The Amish: A People of Preservation, 54 minutes. Mennonite historian/documentary producer John Ruth takes viewers inside the world of the Amish.

Many Grains: Introducing the Mennonite Church, 20 minutes. Introduction to the Mennonite Church.

The Anabaptists (Reformation Overview series, session 5). Highlights Michael and Margaretha Sattler.

The Shakers (Landmarks of Faith series), 46 minutes. A historical overview of the Shakers.

7. The Baptist Tradition

Billy Graham. *Billy Graham* (Great Preachers series) and *Billy Graham . . . Talking with David Frost.*

Candle in the Dark, 97 minutes. Dramatic biography of William Carey.

Charles Colson. Featured in *A Place Called Home; Fighting Back* (The Body series); *Loving God;* and *Evil* (Spiritual Homepage series).

Dangerous Journey. A retelling of John Bunyan's *The Pilgrim's Progress.*

Dispensationalism. For a description, see What We Believe series, session 19. Session 25 defines premillennialism.

Martin Luther King. Featured in several episodes of *Eye on the Prize; Martin's Lament: Religion and Race in America;* and *Martin Luther King, Jr.: The Man and the Dream.*

Puritan New England (Landmarks of Faith series), 48 minutes. Uncover the stories of Anne Hutchinson, Roger Williams, and the true story of the Salem Witch Trials.

Tony Campolo. Interviews with Campolo are featured in the Great Preachers series and Faces on Faith series. For a list of videos with Campolo's many presentations, contact TRAVARCA.

8. The Methodist Tradition

Methodist Camp Meetings (Landmarks of Faith series), 48 minutes. Documentary presents the history of several camp meeting sites and shows how they matured into soul-restoring retreats.

William Willimon, 25 minutes. Willimon is interviewed in this episode of the Great Preachers series.

9. The Holiness and Pentecostal Traditions

Pentecostalism: Caribbean Christmas (Introduction to World Religions series), 15 minutes. Focuses on Christmas celebrations on Barbados. History traced to minister W. J. Seymore and California.

10. Nondenominational Christianity

Fighting Back (The Glory and the Power: Fundamentalisms Observed series), 58 minutes. Opening program of this three-part series explores diverse aspects of Christian fundamentalism in the United States.

An Inside Look at the Willow Creek Seeker Service: Show Me the Way, 116 minutes. Live recording of seeker service. Includes dialogue with Bill Hybels, Nancy Beach, and Lee Strobel.

An Inside Look at the Willow Creek Worship Service: Building a New Community, 116 minutes. In addition to the complete worship service, this video features a dialogue with Bill Hybels, Nancy Beach, and Lee Strobel.

Mine Eyes Have Seen the Glory series. Focuses on the face of evangelical Christianity in the United States. Three-part series includes *America's Folk Religion, The Making of a Subculture,* and *Coming of Age.*

Internet Resources

Note: While all of the following websites were up and running at the time this leader's guide was printed, some sites may no longer be available or may have changed their address.

The Yearbook of American and Canadian Churches: www.ElectronicChurch.org.

Offers links to other sites of general interest to the study of denominations and churches, including the following:

- www.Christianity.about.com/religion/Christianity
  Ad-sponsored website with an evangelical focus. Has a section for Christian teens.

- www.academicinfo.net/Christian.html
  A service of the University of Washington. Locates and lists churches in the United States and Canada.

- www.adherents.com
  Offers statistics of all kinds and lists of famous adherents of various denominations.

- www.allinone.crossdaily.com
  All-in-one Christian Index. Ad-sponsored. Offers all kinds of stuff from clip art to Bible quizzes; also lists other Christian websites.

- www.arda.tm
  American Religion Data Archive, a service provided by the Lilly Foundation. You can enter in the area in which you live and see a map and graph of the various denominational memberships of your location—United States only.

- www.belief.net
  Ad-sponsored site covers all faiths, not just Christianity. Click on "Belief-o-matic" feature to take a quiz that will tell you what denomination you should join, based on your religious beliefs and views.

- www.crosssearch.com
  Locate denomination-specific websites. Click on churches and denominations, then check out both the issues and the denominations categories.

- www.forministry.com
  Sponsored by American Bible Society. Provides a church finder search engine. Enter your location and the denomination you are interested in and it will tell you which churches in that denomination are in your area. United States and Canada searches available.

- www.crosswalk.com
  Claims to be the largest Christian directory on the Web. Offers Bible study, prayer groups, news, and links to other sites.

- www.allexperts.com
  Allows visitors to e-mail questions about a denomination or tradition to a volunteer within that church. Depending on the "expert," the quality of answers can vary substantially.

- www.yahoo.com and www.yahoo.ca
  Yahoo search engine. Click your way through the following categories: society and culture, then religion and spirituality, then faiths and practices, then Christianity. From this category you can further refine your search by region, by churches, and by denomination.

In addition to this list, be sure check out the websites for various denominations suggested in the participant newspapers and in the sessions in this leader's guide.

Stewardship Suggestion

Your denomination may have a mission or word-and-deed ministry that partners with other denominations or Christian traditions, such as a joint AIDS relief effort in South Africa or new church development in the former Soviet republics. Your own congregation may also be involved in a local ecumenical ministry—such as a literacy program or a food pantry—with other churches in your area. Consider challenging the group to provide financial and physical support for such a ministry. For example, your group could sort food or prepare back-to-school packages for a food ministry. Reinforce the universal call to share the gospel of God's love by helping your group see a place where that is being done.

Toward a Theological Perspective

How can we help participants to evaluate the bewildering array of Christian denominations?

We might start by looking at Jesus' prayer recorded in John 17. When the time had come for Jesus to return to his Father by way of the cross, he prayed for three essentials to enable them survive and flourish as God's people:

- protection from the world (v. 11) and from the evil one (v. 15).
- to be set apart by the truth of God's Word (v. 17).
- to be one as Jesus and the Father are one (v. 22).

Has Jesus' prayer for the church been answered?

Sort of.

- God has protected the church so well that it has spread the good news throughout the world. But in many places, God's people continue to endure horrible persecution.
- The church in many places continues to faithfully proclaim, celebrate, and obey the Word of God. But false teaching, worldliness, and lack of devotion to God continue to plague us.
- Christians increasingly recognize that believers of all backgrounds and denominations belong to one Body. But the church is still fractured into hundreds of different groups that have a hard time working together as a real family.

Why do we still have this deep fragmentation that keeps us from clearly showing the world our unity in Christ? It's not because God isn't providing. It's because we're still human:

17

- We can't agree with each other on what the Bible teaches in regard to some finer points of Christian teaching.
- We allow those (smaller) doctrinal differences to overshadow the overwhelming unity we have in our common and shared confession.
- We allow racism, ethnocentrism, personal preferences, and generational differences to build walls that isolate us from each other.

Sadly, our zeal for remaining in God's truth so easily makes us sin against the unity that Jesus prayed for. Conversely, our deep desire for unity in Christ easily makes us water down the truth of the gospel.

In spite of all that, we see the power of God's Spirit working wonders in bringing Jesus' prayer to fulfillment. The Spirit even uses our failures in the process!

- Our differences in interpreting God's Word keep us always testing our beliefs to be sure that we're not all headed in the wrong direction. Nothing gets our noses back into Scripture like a good doctrinal dustup.
- Each of our different denominations and brands of Christianity make their own unique contribution to God's kingdom.
- The endless variety of local expressions of the Christian faith appeal to a wider variety of people who might otherwise never have been joined to God's people.

What does this mean for the way you'll want to present the major denominations to your group? You'll want to celebrate and learn from the God-given strengths of each denomination and frankly point out what you perceive to be their weaknesses. You'll want to emphasize our intrinsic unity as God's family without soft-peddling our significant differences. Finally, you'll want to use this survey as a means of encouraging participants to work in harmony with fellow Christians of all stripes and colors as we all contribute our denomination's own unique spiritual gifts to the mix. Show how to celebrate unity while staying firmly and fully in God's truth. That's how we can be a real answer to Jesus' prayer.

—Bob DeMoor
Editor-in-Chief
Faith Alive Christian Resources

If You Are Using This Course with Adults or Young Adults

At the end of every session you will find ways to adapt this material to use with adults and young adults, who, of course, are at very different places in spiritual development from teens. You'll want to keep in mind that people learn about faith in the following developmental steps:

- **Experienced faith:** Personal experience forms the beginning foundations of our spirituality. For instance, we know that God is a loving parent because we experience parental love as children.
- **Affiliated faith:** By having a place in the Christian community or family of God, we learn that faith involves relationships with others. We see how those relationships are lived out as others model them. For instance, a young child learns what it means to be "giving" by seeing adults give in response to a need in their church.
- **Searching faith:** A time of questioning and sorting leads to acceptance of faith. We come to decide for ourselves what we are going to believe. Most teens are in this stage; they use challenges to help them make these crucial distinctions for themselves. Some young adults are still defining their faith this way.

- **Owned faith:** We have come to a place where we know what we believe and now can work on making that faith meaningful. We learn to share our faith with others and continue to search for new ways to express and understand our faith. Most of the adults in your group will be at this stage of faith formation.

As you help adults discuss and learn this material, you'll discover that some will be more eager to challenge the ideas presented while others will find it easier to appreciate and explore them. Encourage all members of your group to use this course as a way to refine and enrich what they believe.

Finally, most adults will have had prior experience with some of these faith traditions. When you begin your study of each, be sure to ask who has first-hand knowledge and experience. Invite these persons to share with the group what they know, to illustrate and inform. Their experience will significantly enrich your sessions.

The Orthodox Churches

Scripture/Confession	1 Timothy 3:16; Revelation 5:9-14; Nicene Creed
Session Focus	The Reformed family of churches is part of the Western Christian tradition; another large part of Christianity is represented by those who celebrate their faith in the Orthodox Eastern Christian tradition. Mystery is a key faith distinctive of the Orthodox churches.
Session Goals	• to explain how Christianity is shaped by two distinctive faith expressions, both of which claim the apostolic tradition • to identify mystery as a key distinctive of this faith tradition • to describe the basics of Orthodox theology and worship, noting similarities to and differences from our own faith tradition • to tell how the Orthodox churches came to North America • to celebrate the oneness of the church in Christ Jesus
Key Distinctive of This Faith Tradition	To the average North American, Eastern Orthodox is a confusing name for a Christian tradition. Are there Eastern Orthodox in the same way that there are Southern Baptists? Even if we know that Eastern refers to the split between the Eastern and Western churches of the Roman Empire in the eleventh century, we may be confused about the word *Orthodox*. We may think of orthodoxy and wonder if these churches are more conservative than others. Actually, *orthodox* means "true belief." Eastern churches earned the right to be described as Orthodox through their leadership in the early years of the Christian Church. During that time, churches were struggling to define the meaning of true belief in Christ. Who was Christ? God, but not really human? Human, but not really God? Human and God, but not one person? Theological battles raged over these questions. Leaders of the Eastern churches—Alexandria in Egypt, Antioch in Syria, Jerusalem in Palestine, and Constantinople in Turkey—called the seven church councils together that debated the issues and determined the correct doctrines of the church. To be Orthodox, then, is to claim a historic and theological legacy in the Christian Church. This distinction aside, the Orthodox tradition remains something of a mystery to most of us. Their ancient worship is shrouded in incense and dimly lit by candles; their beliefs are expressed in icons, creeds, and prayers instead of systematic theologies and catechisms. In fact, mystery is very much at the heart of Orthodox worship and theology. After all, what could be more mysterious than a God—the Creator of the entire universe—who chooses to become a human being? What kind of God can be a Trinity? Why would this God choose to love us so sacrificially? How is it possible that ordinary bread and wine become the body and blood of our Savior? According to the Orthodox, these questions are unanswerable. As Christians, they say, we are simply to accept the truths of God's nature and actions on our behalf with thanksgiving and joy.

This emphasis on mystery, this willingness to accept what we can never truly know is a little unsettling to those of us in the Reformed tradition. Why? First, because we are so heavily influenced by our twenty-first century emphasis on technology and information. We want answers—and the Internet, along with a host of related technologies, scrambles to provide them. Second, our own Reformed/Presbyterian faith tradition—while not negating mystery—tends to emphasize and value knowledge. We want to know, as exactly as we can, what God is like, who Jesus is, how the Spirit works to bring us to salvation. We value a clear and systematic theology, a way of knowing that finds expression in memorable catechisms, detailed confessional statements, and a strong system of Christian education.

Yet the truth remains that God is so much bigger than we are that we can never really know all there is to know of God and God's love for us. Paul writes to Timothy, "Beyond all question, the mystery of godliness is great" (1 Tim. 3:16). The Orthodox tradition reminds us that at the heart of our faith is simple, grateful wonder for who God is and what God has done.

Materials

Leader
- Bible
- Newsprint, marker
- Participant newspaper: The Orthodox Churches
- "Spot the Dog" (p. 31), overhead or photocopies for each group member
- Listing of local Orthodox churches from newspaper, yellow pages, or Internet
- Optional: overhead or large sketch of the blank Christian family tree (see reproducible page at the end of this session, p. 32)

Key website you may want to check for more information:
www.oca.org (Orthodox Church in America)

Participants
- Bible
- Participant newspaper: The Orthodox Churches
- Photocopy of blank Christian family tree (p. 32), one per student
- Optional: notecards, one per participant for option for steps 1 and 2
- Optional: copy of schedule for the course

Session at a Glance

Step 1: We take a quick look at the course and its schedule (5 minutes).

Step 2: We use "Spot the Dog" to get at the idea of mystery (5 minutes).

Step 3: We use the newspaper to look at an icon and to learn about the theology and worship of the Orthodox churches (20-25 minutes).

Step 4: We use the main article on page 1 and the "Christian family tree" to look at how the Orthodox churches came to North America (10-15 minutes).

Step 5: We wrap up the session by reciting the Nicene Creed in unison, looking at the unity of the church, and reading a description of the future church from Revelation 5 (10 minutes).

Note: We suggest a minimum of an hour for these sessions. You'll find that you can easily expand that time, even adding an extra session on each faith tradition, using the unread articles in the newspaper and the ideas in the course introduction. If you must cut the time to, say, forty-five minutes, you'll need to omit some of the activities we suggest and shorten others. **In this session, for example, you could omit the introductions in step 1, use the timesaving options suggested at the end of steps 2 and 4, and use only the Trinity prayer from step 6.**

<table>
<tr><td>Step 1</td><td>

Getting Started

The appearance of your meeting room can make a huge difference in the enthusiasm of your group. Please see "Thinking Inside the Room" on pages 9-10 for suggestions on how to make your room say, "This is going to be an exciting course!" Add some refreshments and you'll be off to a great start.

If this is your first meeting with the group, see the option below this step for a fun way to get started.

Talk a bit about the course and explain what you'll be studying and discussing together. Show them a few of the ten newspapers, anything you've set up in the room, and talk about and/or hand out the course schedule. Announce field trip dates and any other assignments you're making for the group. (See the ideas in "Getting Outside the Room," pp. 10-11, for ways to enhance the course with outside activities.)

</td></tr>
</table>

First Meeting?

First time you're meeting as a group? If so, spend a few minutes getting to know each other. Pass out notecards and have everyone list their name and the title of their all-time favorite movie (or favorite TV show or favorite food or something fun like what's under their bed). Then collect the cards and read them aloud without mentioning the name on the card. Let the group guess who they think wrote it. Have fun—and learn about what your group likes. Don't forget to make a card about yourself too!

<table>
<tr><td>Step 2</td><td>

Introducing the Idea of Mystery

Distribute copies of "Spot the Dog" (see p. 31) or show an overhead of the same drawing. (Do not identify the picture as "Spot the Dog"!) Ask the group to silently study it and decide what it's a picture of. After everyone has guessed or failed to guess, use a marker to highlight the lines of the dog.

</td></tr>
</table>

Ask questions like these:

- **How is this picture mysterious?** (We didn't quite know what we were looking for; we saw but didn't understand; we knew part of the truth but not all of it.)

- **In what way is our Christian faith mysterious?** (We know only some of the truth about who God is; we can't fully understand God: for example, we can't really explain how Jesus could be fully human and fully divine; we don't understand why God allows bad things to happen; there are lots of questions for which we don't have answers.) You may want to have someone read 1 Timothy 3:16 aloud.

Explain that the oldest part of the Christian church, which includes the churches of the New Testament, is part of a Christian faith tradition that celebrates the mystery of God in its beliefs and worship.

Option: Timesaver

Instead of using "Spot the Dog," distribute notecards and have everyone write one thing about any aspect of the Christian faith that is mysterious to them—maybe something they'd like to ask Jesus about when they get to see him someday. Collect the (unsigned) cards and read them aloud. Talk about the ways our faith is mysterious.

Step 3

Icons, Beliefs, Worship

Distribute the newspaper on the Orthodox churches. Remember, you should not attempt to read the entire newspaper in a one-hour session! Instead, this session will use four articles, with references to others along the way. Participants can take the newspaper home at the end of the session and read additional articles there, if they wish to do so.

You'll want to experiment with different ways of reading the various articles. Sometimes you can ask for volunteers to take turns reading the articles aloud. At other times a silent reading may be the quickest and most effective. From time to time you may also want group members to pair off or work in small groups, reading the article silently or to each other and then doing various activities as a group.

Icons

Ask the group to turn to "Icons: A Door to Heaven" on page 4. Ask for volunteers to read the short article to the group. Then take a moment to have everyone look closely at the icon in "An Icon Up Close." They should look at the picture *without* reading the explanation in the article. Then ask questions like the following:

- **What biblical scene is being pictured here?** (You may want to take a moment to describe the scene from Genesis 18).

Have someone read the explanation of the icon. Ask:

- **How is this icon a little like the picture "Spot the Dog"?** (You need to look closely to "see through it," to understand the whole picture; there's an element of mystery.)

- **Orthodox Christians use icons to help them pray. How could an icon do this?**

- **Why do you suppose most people in the Reformed/Presbyterian tradition don't use icons today?** (Icons are not part of our tradition; they are new to us, untried, and may even be somewhat threatening to some. For example, we might worry that the icon itself would become the object of our worship or that it would somehow come between us and God. In that case, the icon would become a barrier to our prayers rather than an aid.)

You may also want to use the questions at the end of the article in the newspaper.

What This Church Believes
Refer the group to "What This Church Believes" on page 2 and read it aloud together (ask for a different volunteer or have a few take turns). Ask the group to underline any statements they don't understand or that they would like to talk about further. Review the article using questions like these:

- **What does it mean to be apostolic?** (Practicing Christianity as taught by the apostles.)

- **Why do the Orthodox say that God is a mystery?** (No one can completely understand God.)

- **If *ortho* means "true" (an orthodontist tries to give you "true" teeth), then what does it mean to be Orthodox?** (It means to have true belief, to honor the apostolic faith.) Point out that the word *orthodox* also means "true worship" or "true glory." *Dox*—see it in *doxology*—means "praise" or "worship."

- **What's similar to our beliefs? What's different?** (Similarities include belief in the Trinity (see the Nicene Creed), in its work of salvation, in living a life of obedience and service. Differences include a strong emphasis on the mystery of God, the use of seven sacraments rather than two, an emphasis on unity with God achieved through spiritual disciplines.) You may also want to mention a difference in our understanding of atonement: the Orthodox understand the atonement as Christ's great victory that sets us free from sin and death; our faith tradition sees it as Christ's substitutionary sacrifice that pays the debt of sin that we are unable to pay for ourselves—a more "legal" approach.

If time permits, call attention to "Who Leads This Church?" and the system of leadership (priest, deacons, bishop, and so on) of these churches.

Worship
Ask the group to read (silently) the article "Worship: Inside an Orthodox Church." As they read, they should highlight or underline any features they like about worshiping in an Orthodox Church. After the reading, ask:

- **What did you mark? Would worshiping in an Orthodox congregation be appealing to you? Why or why not?**

- **What is similar to our worship? What is different?** (You may want to re-read the paragraph beginning: "Orthodox worship engages all the senses. . . ." Note also the emphasis on icons and mystery in the Orthodox tradition.

If you're planning on taking the group to visit an Orthodox church, use the above article and discussion to generate enthusiasm and help the group know what to expect.

<table>
<tr><td>Step 4</td><td>

History and Family Tree

Have the group turn to the article "From Pentecost Sunday to the Orthodox Church Down the Street" (p. 1). Take turns reading it aloud (if you're short on time, see the option at the end of this step).

Stop after reading the second paragraph of the "East Versus West" section, the one about the Catholic church splitting in two. Distribute blank "Christian family tree" pages that you've photocopied from page 32. Have the group fill in their family trees, adding the writing shown on the diagram on page 4 of the newspaper.

If you've made an enlargement of the family tree or have built a three-dimensional model (see p. 10), display that now and fill in the names and dates for this week. Another possibility is to make a transparency and use an overhead projector. Explain that you'll be adding to the family tree each week. Collect the family trees at the end of each session (have participants write their names on their copy).

Continue reading the remainder of the article. Finish by pointing out the "Facts and Figures" box on page 1, noting that there are approximately five million Orthodox Christians living in the United States and Canada today. Supply information about any local or nearby Orthodox churches, telling what denomination they are affiliated with and where they are located. Are any of them "the church down the street"?

Option: Timesaver

If you don't have time to read "From Pentecost Sunday to the Church Down the Street," skip the article and use only the timeline on page 2 and the map on page 1 as you briefly describe the events associated with the dates. Do the family tree exercise as described above.

</td></tr>
</table>

Step 5

Wrap-up

Ask the group to reflect on this question:

- **What can we learn from this faith tradition that could help our own faith grow?** (By the way, this is a good question to ask throughout this course. It helps build appreciation for the faith group being studied. Highlight a renewed appreciation of the mystery of God, the key distinctive of this faith tradition.)

Have the group turn to "Pause Button" on page 4. Read the brief explanation of the Nicene Creed that's found there, then read all or part of the creed in unison, as time permits. (You may want to show the group where the Nicene Creed is found in your church's hymnal).

Ask the group to go back to the fourth line from the end: "We believe in one holy catholic and apostolic church." Ask: **How is it possible that all the various kinds of churches and denominations can be one holy**

catholic and apostolic church? (You might need to point out that *catholic* means universal and *apostolic* means the church born at Pentecost in Acts.)

Help the group briefly define some key elements of the Christian faith that all believers hold in common: worship of the triune God, the gift of salvation from sin through the work of Jesus on the cross, acceptance of the Bible as the Word of God, carrying out the command to love our neighbor as ourselves, a calling to a life of faithful discipleship, and the hope of our eternal future with God. You may want to use Robert DeMoor's analogy from *Quest of Faith:* if the church is the body of Christ, think of individual congregations as the cells, and denominations as the organs or bones.

Comment that during our study over the next weeks we will be noticing a lot of differences between the kinds of Christian churches, but that we should never forget what we all confess and believe together.

Conclude by asking the group to turn to Revelation 5:9-14. Ask the group to read in unison the song of the saints (in quotation marks) in these verses. Read the other verses yourself. Before beginning, explain that this is what the church will be like someday when it is truly one holy catholic and apostolic church.

Conclude by reading the **Orthodox Prayer** in unison from page 4:

My hope is the Father,
My refuge is the Son,
My protection is the Holy Spirit,
Holy Trinity,
Glory to Thee.

If your group enjoys singing, you may also want to sing the doxology "Glory Be to the Father," a song of joy that has been sung since the earliest days of the Christian church. Today we sing it in English rather than chant it in Greek, but the words continue to help us celebrate the one-God-in-three we worship.

Before your group leaves, please encourage them to read more of the newspaper at home. Call their attention to articles they didn't read in class but might enjoy reading at home.

Suggest that group members save the newspapers as a quick and easy guide to the major faith traditions in North America.

Looking Ahead to the Next Session

Give yourself plenty of time to review the resource on Roman Catholicism. You may want to do some further reading on some of its faith practices. Check the websites listed in the resource. Another possibility is to contact a local Catholic Church and ask if they have any booklets that explain Catholicism to Protestants.

Nearly all communities have a local Catholic Church, and we highly recommend a visit to one in your community (after your study of session 2). If attending worship there would make some in your group uncomfortable, ask the parish associate to arrange a tour and conversation with the priest or deacon.

You may want to borrow some examples of the following items associated with prayer practices in the Roman Catholic tradition: rosary, prayer candle, figure of a saint, or prayer card. A Catholic religious store would carry inexpensive versions of these items.

1. Meditating on an Icon
Make a color transparency of the icon in the student newspaper and project it
in your room. Light a candle or two, dim the lights, and lead your group in a
time of meditation using the icon. Remind the group that this is an icon of
the Trinity—God is pictured as the three persons of the Trinity seated around a
table at which you have been invited to take a seat. This meditation is an
opportunity to lift the mind and heart to God, to be in God's presence and
reflect on God's names, persons, power, and love. The icon is merely a point to
focus those thoughts as we figuratively put ourselves at that table and reflect
on what it means to be seated there.

Have the group sit silently in meditation after you introduce that time with
one of the following Scripture passages: Psalm 36:5-9; John 14:1-3; Isaiah
25:6-9; or a single verse like 2 Corinthians 13:14 or Psalm 34:8. Then say, **Sit in
quietness in the presence of the icon and open your heart to God.**

Allow for about five minutes of silent meditation and then have the group
close in unison with the words "Glory to you, O Lord, glory to you."

2. Field Trip
Attending worship at an Orthodox Church would be a great learning experience for your group. Consult *How to Be a Perfect Stranger* (see p. 12) to prepare
your group for the experience. Also review the diagram of the interior of an
Orthodox Church in the participant newspaper, and check "Getting Outside
the Room" on page 10. Be sure your group understands that only Orthodox
Christians may participate in the Eucharist; your group will only be watching
this sacrament. At the end of the liturgy, the worshiping body is offered a
piece of blessed bread called the *antidoron* which all those present, no matter
their faith tradition, are invited to receive as an expression of Christian fellowship and love.

Afterward, discuss the experience using questions like the following:

• **What new or unusual experiences did you have? How did you
feel about it?**

• **What senses were involved in worship? How did that affect your
experience?**

• **Were there elements of this worship that you wish were part of
our worship services? What elements of worship help you worship best? What did you think was the aim or theme of worship
as it was communicated by the liturgy?**

3. Icon Talk
Find a local art teacher or artist to talk about icons and how faith and art work
together in worship. Find out if your local art museum has any icons and
arrange a docent guided tour for your group if it does.

4. I Believe
This session closes by looking at a creed. Have the group note that that creeds
are both personal and communal statements of faith: they begin with the
words "I believe" or "we believe." Have kids work in small groups to write their
own creed. It should consist of "we believe" statements about the following:

- God
- what God does for people
- salvation and Jesus
- the Holy Spirit
- how God works in our lives
- the church

Have the groups write their creed on sheets of newsprint. Compare the statements and see what's similar and what's different. You may want to use some of the statements as part of your closing devotions during this course.

5. Video Reminders
TRAVARCA offers several videos on the Orthodox churches that you could use during an extra session. Check the list on page 13 for details and ordering information.

If Group Members Are Adults or Young Adults	**Step 1:** Instead of or in addition to the movie quiz, you might want to ask the group to share why they are interested in the course and what they hope to learn. You'll also want to ask the group what Christian traditions they have had experience with in the past. This can help you plan which sessions they might contribute to in a special way. Someone who has had a Lutheran upbringing, for example, may be able to help you lead the discussion on the Lutheran tradition.

Step 2: You will probably want to drop the "Spot the Dog" activity with adults and use the option instead. Be aware that adults may define mystery more subtly than teens. They are able to recognize ambiguity as one of its definitions, as opposed to a simpler definition of lack of knowledge. The mystery of Orthodox thought and worship is more than simply an awareness of the immensity of God that places us in a state of wonder; it is also the extremes that we hold in tension when we confess Jesus as human and divine.

Steps 3 and 4: As you work through the content of the major articles in the resource, ask the group to share what they know about Orthodox churches. Some may have worshiped in a church or attended a wedding or funeral in this tradition. Use your group's life experiences to illustrate the text.

Also, with adults or young adults, you should be able to go into greater depth on all questions of similarities and differences between the Orthodox faith tradition and your own.

You may also want to take up the issue that helped split the church into East and West—the so-called *filoque* clause of the Nicene Creed. The Western Church insisted on an expanded version of the line that confesses that the Holy Spirit proceeds from the Father. It taught that the Holy Spirit proceeds from the Father *and the Son* (Latin: *filoque*). The Orthodox Church refused the addition, arguing that the Son and the Spirit were two separate and distinct gifts from the Father alone. That doctrinal difference still divides Western and Orthodox churches today.

Step 5: Session Wrap-up. You may want to add more small group dynamics to the session, allowing for more times of intentional sharing and fellowship-building (although these can be present in sessions with youth as well). In today's session, for example, you could end with an extended time of prayer. Share prayer requests with each other. Consider using a format like this one:

- Open with words of praise and thanksgiving, then allow group members to offer items of praise. Leader closes with the words **My hope is the Father.**

- Move to items of confession. Leader closes with the words **My refuge is the Son.**

- Move to requests of need. Leader closes with the words **My protection is the Holy Spirit.**

- End with words of blessing. Leader closes with the words **Holy Trinity, Glory to Thee.**

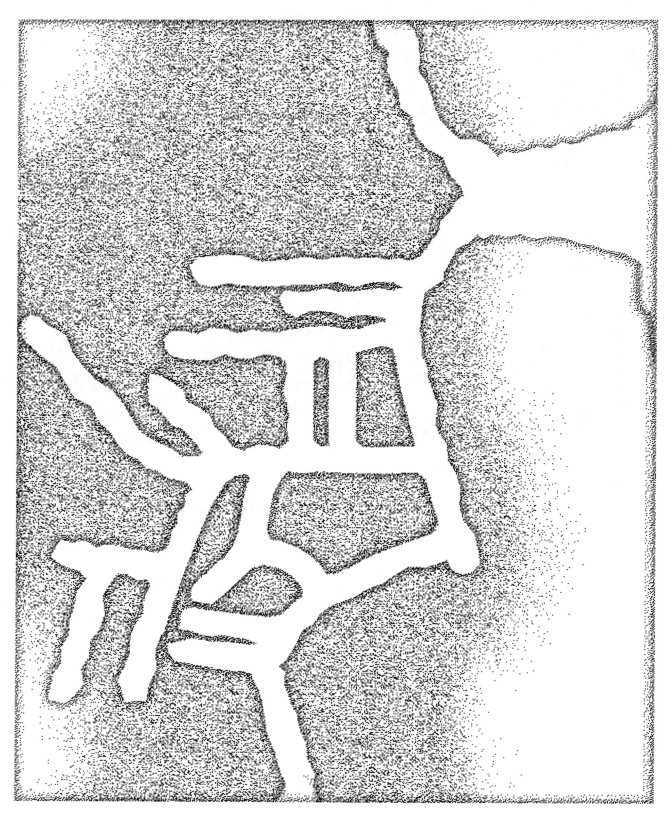

The Roman Catholic Church

2

Scripture/Confession	Ephesians 1:15-18; 2:8-9; 6:18; Heidelberg Catechism, Q&A 55

Session Focus

The Roman Catholic Church is the largest and most influential of all Christian faith traditions. The key distinctive of this faith tradition is an emphasis on acts of personal devotion as a means of continuing the process of grace that God has begun in our lives.

Session Goals

- to appreciate the breadth and diversity of the Catholic Church
- to identify at least three faith practices that are distinct from Protestant traditions
- to appreciate the historical struggle for acceptance by Catholic Christians in North America
- to define sainthood as understood by both Roman Catholic and Protestant traditions
- to see ourselves as "saints"

Key Distinctive of This Faith Tradition

As I am writing this session, the Roman Catholic Church in North America is under heavy attack. Headlines point out the pope's fragile health and speculate how much longer he will be able to lead the church. Newsmagazine cover stories detail the trials of priests accused of sexual crimes and the church's efforts to cover up the scandals. Opinion polls reveal a rising tide of distrust and antipathy by Catholics toward their church. One can't help but wonder what changes the next ten years will bring to the church of Rome. Will this troubled time be an occasion for reform and renewal or one of defensive reaction?

This isn't the first time this faith tradition has come under scrutiny. As Protestants, we know all too well that the Roman Catholic Church has its faults; we have inherited a great legacy from those who sought to reform it centuries ago. In fact, that very history has distanced us from the largest group of Christians in the world. Some 25 percent of North Americans are members of the Catholic Church—more than any other religious group of any kind. And yet for most of our four-hundred-year-old history as a Christian tradition, we Protestants have kept Catholics at arm's length.

Our Reformed tradition still reflects that history. As a child I was told (and believed) that Catholics had invented trick-or-treating as a way to keep us from going to Reformation Day services at our churches; that Catholics practiced idolatry when they put figures of St. Christopher on their dashboards; that it would be better to not marry at all than to marry a Catholic. Even today some Reformed Christians are reluctant to include Catholics in the Christian family tree, viewing them almost as if they were members of a different religion.

It's important to note that some of the most genuine people of faith we may know are members of this church: a young woman who has great compassion for the poor and who wants to be a nun; a wise priest who can teach us much

33

about how to pastor a diverse congregation; a neighbor who models contemplative prayer. The Roman Catholic Church reaches out to new immigrant populations, stabilizes inner cities, and models Christian education. The only Christian church for hundreds of years after Christ left this earth, it is still the single largest—and most influential—Christian group in the world today.

One of our challenges in this session is to look beyond what we know or understand only partially so that we can develop a sincere appreciation for how this tradition carries out the task of being Christ in the world. No Protestant ought to overlook or negate the contributions of Catholicism and Catholics to Christianity throughout the world. Together, Catholics and Protestants of many faith traditions form "one holy catholic church."

On the other hand, we ought not to be ignorant of the distinctives that mark Catholicism and set it off from our own beliefs. In this session we could focus on many such issues: the doctrines of sin and confession, the role of grace in the sacraments, the place of tradition as a source of authority, or the role of apostolic succession. We've chosen instead to focus on the distinctive of *practice*. Why do Catholics *do* that? Why do they pray with rosaries? Why do they light votive candles to saints? Why does a bride present flowers to the virgin Mary in the wedding ceremony? Questions relating to Catholic practices are the kind Protestants—especially young persons—most frequently ask (see, for example, the book *Why Do Catholics Do That?* by Kevin Orlin Johnson). Many of these practices arise out of the great emphasis Catholics place on their personal devotional lives.

Why is being a "good Catholic" defined by what you *do* and not by who you *are?* The distinction lies in a fundamental difference of opinion about what it means to be a Christian. Catholics believe it means that God's grace has begun to work in our life; we continue the process by what we do. In effect, salvation is a joint project between the Christian and God. Jesus' work on the cross took care of the curse of our original state of sin; now we have to recognize and repent of the sins we are individually responsible for.

Reformed Christians believe that God's grace delivers a complete salvation. That means all of our sins are completely forgiven; our lives reflect our acts of thanksgiving in response to that great act of grace. Salvation is God's project, not ours. "For it is by grace you have been saved, through faith—and this not from yourself, it is the gift of God—not by works, so that no one can boast" (Eph. 2:8-9).

An application of this distinction between "doing" and "being" is evident in the different ways Catholic and Reformed Christians view saints. Catholics draw a sharp distinction between saint and sinner. To qualify for sainthood, an individual must have done many good works and even performed miracles (as the participant newspaper notes, a Vatican team has already compiled 35,000 pages documenting Mother Teresa's good works). In the Catholic tradition, saints are not ordinary Christians but persons who are prayed to and held in high esteem because of their exemplary lives.

Reformed believers, on the hand, have erased the distinction between saints and sinners. All Christians are both saints and sinners at the same time. We confess a "communion of the saints." And we are saints not because of what we do but because of who we are in Christ. "Believers one and all, as members of this community (of saints) share in Christ and in all his treasures and gifts" (Heidelberg Catechism, Q&A 55).

Romans 1:7

We will be looking at these distinctions in today's session. But we will also be taking an appreciative look at how much the Roman Catholic Church has contributed to the cause of Christ in the world.

Note: You may want to explain to your group that the word *catholic* is not capitalized when it refers to the universal church of Christ; we are all members of the catholic church. However, Catholic Church refers to the Roman Catholic Church in particular.

Materials

Leader
- Bible
- Participant newspaper: The Roman Catholic Church
- Newsprint, markers
- Listing of local Catholic churches from newspaper, yellow pages, or Internet
- Votive or prayer candle
- Optional: rosary (check a bookstore selling Catholic devotional items)
- Optional: prayer to Saint Jude (from the personal ads in your local newspaper)
- Optional: prayer card or other Catholic devotional item
- Optional: large poster of Christian family tree (see session 1)

Key websites you may want to check for more information:
www.onerock.com (teen e-zine with interesting articles, chat room, weekly polls, "ask the expert," and more)
www.catholic.net (information center on the Catholic faith)

Participants
- Bible
- Participant newspaper: The Roman Catholic Church
- Optional: rosary for each participant

Session at a Glance

Step 1: We use a game to introduce "walking in the shoes" of another Christian tradition, then list questions we have about the Roman Catholic tradition (10 minutes).

Step 2: Working in small groups, we read and summarize articles from the participant newspaper on Catholic history, leadership, worship, and beliefs (20 minutes).

Step 3: We answer questions the group raised at the beginning of the session and use the newspaper to talk about a variety of Catholic devotional practices (15 minutes).

Step 4: We read "Who Is a Good Catholic?" then make a list describing a good Presbyterian or a good Reformed person. We compare our lists with the article we read (10 minutes).

Step 5: We close the session with prayer (3 minutes).

Note: We suggest a minimum of an hour for these sessions. You'll find that you can easily expand that time, even adding an extra session on each faith tradition, using the unread articles in the newspaper and the ideas in the course introduction. If you must cut the time to, say, forty-five minutes, you'll need to omit some of the activities we suggest and shorten others. **In this session, for example, you could omit the shoe game in step 1 and omit step 4.**

Getting Started

Begin by using the following game to introduce the idea of "walking in the shoes" of another Christian tradition.

Have your group form a circle, take off their shoes, and toss them in a pile in the middle. When you give the OK, everyone should grab a pair of shoes (not their own) and put them on. (They don't necessarily have to match; if your group is small, toss in some extra shoes you've brought from home). The last person to get a pair on and tied is "out." Play several rounds—eliminating a pair of shoes each time—until you have a winner—or, if you prefer, just play a few rounds for fun, without declaring a winner.

After the last round, have everyone keep the shoes on and try walking in them. When the laughs and pratfalls are over, ask these questions:

- **What was the game was supposed to demonstrate?**

- **What does it mean to walk in someone's shoes?** (To look at something through another person's eyes, to give another perspective a chance.)

- **What groups of people in our world might appreciate us trying to walk in their shoes?** (Someone living in a war zone in the Middle East; or a poverty-stricken inhabitant of the Third World; or someone suffering from AIDS or racial discrimination; and so on.)

- **Think about other groups of Christians. Should we as Protestants ought to try walking in their shoes? What church do you think we understand the least or are the most confused about?** (You will probably get a variety of answers; suggest Roman Catholics, if the kids don't.)

- **What kinds of discoveries do you think you might make as you learn about the Catholic Church or talk to Catholics? Can you share any you've already experienced?**

What do you know of the Catholic church?

Ask the group what things about the Catholic tradition are hard to understand or confusing. What questions do they have about this tradition? List them on a sheet of newsprint or on an overhead as kids name them. Include some of the following questions on the list, if the group doesn't mention them:

- **Why do Catholics pray to saints?**

- **Why do Catholics pray the rosary? Light votive candles in church? Run ads in newspapers that are prayers to saints?**

- **What do Catholics believe about saints?**

Explain that we'll be returning to our list later in the session to see if our questions were answered.

Option: Christian Family Tree

You may want to use the "Christian family tree" poster you made (see session 1) as a quick review of last week's topic (the Orthodox Church) and as an introduction to the Roman Catholic Church. Participants don't need their copies of the family tree because they do not add any new data this week.

Step 2

Worship, Beliefs, Leadership, History

Distribute the newspaper on the Roman Catholic Church. Divide the group into four smaller groups and assign each one a different article in the resource, as follows:

- "Worship: The Story of Christ" (p. 3)
- "What This Church Believes" (p. 4)
- "Who Leads This Church?" (p. 2)
- "The First Christians" (p. 1)

If your class is very small, it's OK to have one person assigned to each article. Groups may also be of different sizes: larger groups can take the longer articles ("The First Christians" and "Worship: The Story of Christ").

Have each group read its assigned article; they may want to take turns reading aloud within their groups or just each read their assigned article silently. After the reading, groups should do a "handshake"—that is, come up with one summary point for each finger on one hand. Point out to them the questions you've come up with as a group and remind them to look for answers in their articles. The group should agree on a single "handshake" of five key points it wants to present. Group members may jot down their summary points on newsprint or underline them in their article.

After ten minutes or so, have the groups present their "handshake" of five key points about their article. Group members may take turns presenting their points or choose one person to be the reporter. As groups present, be sure the rest of the class locates the article in their newspaper. You may want them to underline key points in the articles as the group identifies them.

Following are some summary statements containing items you may want to mention if the groups don't:

1. Worship: The Story of Christ
- All forms of worship and devotion—if they do not hinder the gospel—are allowable.
- Catholic worship comes from third-century Roman imperial customs.
- The focus of worship is the Mass.
- God's grace is administered only through the sacraments of the church.
- The most significant part of God's grace is Christ's death on the cross. You can add here that the act of genuflection (bowing toward the altar) is one you'll see often in a Catholic Church. It is a sign of respect, like making the sign of the cross that accompanies it, and obeisance to the physical presence of Christ in the room (see option on page 38).

Take a couple of minutes to look at the sketch of the inside of a Catholic Church (p. 3) This is especially important if the group is going to visit a Catholic Church.

2. What This Church Believes

- The pope is the spiritual descendent of the apostle Peter.
- Tradition is an important addition to Scripture in deciding doctrine.
- We have to repair the damage our sins cause.
- If there were no church, the world would not know Christ.
- Purgatory is a place of purification where souls go before they can enter heaven.

3. Who Leads This Church?

- The priest is the primary leader of a local parish.
- A bishop is the leader of a diocese or group of churches.
- An archbishop is a leader of the bishops.
- A cardinal is an advisor to the pope.
- The pope is the father or "papa" of the church and as a direct descendent of the apostle Peter is infallible when he makes an official pronouncement.

4. The First Christians

- The first Christians in North America were Catholics.
- Immigration in the nineteenth century brought millions of Catholics to our countries.
- Catholics were considered a threat and were treated badly until the twentieth century.
- Catholics are the largest Christian group in North America.
- New Catholic immigrant groups are Hispanic or Asian.

You may want to take a quick look at the "Timeline" (p. 2) and at the "Facts and Figures" on page 1.

Option: Sign of the Cross

As part of your discussion on worship, teach the group how to make the sign of the cross. Ask them, of course, to do this with reverence and respect. Say something like this: **If you were a Catholic entering a Catholic Church, you would begin by dipping your hand in holy water, then touching your forehead, chest, left shoulder, and right shoulder, finally folding your hands together. You could also add the words "In the name of the Father and of the Son and of the Holy Spirit" as you touch each point of the cross.**

Option: Questions About the Mass

If students had questions about the Mass, read "Experiencing the Mass: A Protestant/Catholic Teen Speaks Out" (p. 3). Ask the group what they find attractive about the Mass. How is it similar to and different from our celebration of the Lord's Supper?

Step 3

Questions About Catholic Practices

Refer back to the list of questions your group formed at the beginning of the session. Are any still unanswered? Answer any still remaining, referring to articles in the newspaper as necessary.

Point out that one distinctive of the Catholic tradition is a strong emphasis on personal devotional practices. Address the questions you've planted on the practice of rosaries, votive candles, and prayer to saints. Refer to these articles and illustrations from the newspaper as discussion helps:

- "Honoring Our Mother" and picture of rosary (p. 4). Use this article and captioned illustration of a rosary for a discussion of praying to Mary and using the rosary. If you've managed to locate a rosary, show it to the class now and demonstrate how to use it.

- "What a Saint!" (p. 4). Explain that Catholics believe that we may pray to saints so that they will mediate for us, presenting our requests to God. Since Mary is the greatest saint of all, worship directed to her is the most popular. Catholics believe that saints pray for persons still on earth and act as their advocate before the throne of God, bringing their petitions and representing their cause.

Light a votive candle, explaining that these are lit in Catholic churches and placed in front of a statue of a particular saint like Saint Jude (the saint of lost causes). As long as the candle burns, the prayer is being spoken. Newspaper prayers and prayer cards function the same way: whenever such a prayer is read by anyone, it is being prayed. Then ask questions like these:

- **What could be comforting about believing that a saint is praying for something or someone you care about?** (You may want to point out that there is a saint of test-taking—Joseph of Cupertino—and a saint of teens—Maria Goretti—and, of course, a saint of love—Valentine.)

- **Do Protestants believe that some human beings are saints?** (Prompt them to remember that this is part of the Apostles' Creed.)

- **What does it mean to say, "I believe in the communion of saints?" Who are saints, according to our (Protestant) understanding?** (See "Key Distinctive of This Faith Tradition," pp. 33-35, for comments. You may also want to refer to Ephesians 1:15-18 and Q&A 55 of the Heidelberg Catechism.)

- **How could learning about the lives of the saints—as defined by Catholics—help us?** (People of exceptional faith, whether Catholic or Protestant, can serve as models for us; they can inspire and encourage us.)

- **Do we pray *to* the saints or *with* the saints or *for* the saints, according to the Bible?** (Ephesians 6:18 indicates that we pray for all the saints, that is, for all believers. And, of course, we also pray *with* the saints whenever we pray with other believers.)

- **How are you a saint?**

Conclude this section by commenting that behind the Catholic practices of praying to saints, of praying the rosary, of penance, of lighting votive candles to saints is their understanding of salvation. Catholics believe that God has begun to work with grace in our lives; we must now continue the process. You could think of salvation as grace *plus* our own acts of devotions and good deeds. Reformed folks believe that God's grace *alone* is sufficient for our complete salvation. Ephesians 2:8-9 is the classic text on this. Do not go into detail on this point right now—next week we'll study Lutheranism with its great emphasis on "salvation by grace through faith."

Option: Using the Rosary
Provide a rosary for each group member. Then recite a decade—an Our Father and ten Hail Marys—together.

Option: Find a Saint

Locate a list of the saints of United States or Canada and share this with the group. See if any of the saints come from your part of the country. Or get a copy of *Sister Wendy's Book of Saints* and let the group find out more about the patron saints of various causes. You may also want to visit the website www.saint.catholic.org to locate some examples of saints.

Step 4	## Who Is a Good Catholic?

If you haven't already, ask the group if they have Catholic neighbors or friends (or families). If so, ask: **How does this person "practice" being a Catholic?** If your group doesn't know any Catholics, share what you know of Catholic practice as you have observed it or experienced it.

Direct the group to the short article on page 3, "Who Is a Good Catholic?" and have someone read it aloud. Assign kids to their group again and have them create a similar list titled "A Good Reformed Christian" or "A Good Presbyterian." Give the groups a sheet of newsprint and a marker to write their list. After five minutes, bring them together and have them compare their lists to the items listed in the sidebar. Talk about some of the similarities and differences between their lists and what's mentioned in the sidebar.

If time is running out, work on making a list together, rather than working in groups. If you have plenty of time, you might try editing all the small group lists into a single list together.

A Reformed/Presbyterian list might include some of the following: believe in Jesus Christ as Savior and Lord; attend church regularly; attend church education programs, youth group, and so on; be active in some form of service/ministry; pray and read the Bible every day; receive communion each time it is celebrated; practice stewardship; only date (and marry) other Christians; have your children baptized; follow the Ten Commandments; share the gospel in both word and deed.

Step 5	## Wrap-up

Here are some suggestions for closing the session:

- Lead the group in prayer using the words of the hymn "For All the Saints Who Showed Your Love" written by John Bell. You can find this song in *Sing! A New Creation* #195, (available from Faith Alive Christian Resources). Your group may enjoy singing it together often.

- Have group members make the sign of cross (see option to step 3).

- Have the group say in unison the prayer of Brother Roger of the Taizé community (see "Pause Button," p. 4).

  Lord Christ,
  at times we are like strangers on this earth,
  taken aback by all the violence, the harsh oppositions.
  Like a gentle breeze, you breathe upon us the Spirit of peace.

Transfigure the deserts of our doubts,
and so prepare us to be bearers of reconciliation
wherever you place us,
until the day when a hope of peace
dawns in our world. Amen.

Encourage everyone to read the rest of the newspaper at home this week. Call attention to some articles that you think might be interesting for group members to read on their own.

Looking Ahead to the Next Session

Review the newspaper on the Lutheran tradition and read the session plan. Decide which articles in the paper and which steps in the session you'll use with your group. If you have time, you might want to check out the ELCA website for additional information.

To add some (optional) variety to the session, consider asking a couple of "future teachers" in your group to serve as presenters and discussion leaders for two articles in the student newspaper. Ask someone to read and summarize "Here I Stand" and another person to do the same for "Luther's Rose." Your presenters may be as creative as they wish. For example, they could stage an interview with Luther, having another student ask him some prepared questions. Or presenters could simply summarize their articles, calling attention to what they consider to be key statements.

The above is strictly an option (see option to step 2 in session 3).

You may also want to check TRAVARCA listings (see p. 14) on Luther's life or the beginning of the Reformation as a way to present some of the historical theology of this tradition.

If you're a Lake Wobegon fan, you may want to pick out a favorite Garrison Keillor story to play for the group (see "Want to Read More?" p. 4).

Extending the Session

1. Case Studies
Give your group the following case studies to discuss (you may want to have them work in small groups to arrive at their response, then share it with the rest of the class).

- Your best friend informs you that she is dating a guy she met at work. He's Catholic. She asks you, "Do you think it makes any difference that he's Catholic and I'm Protestant? We're both Christians, aren't we?" How would you respond?

- A member of your youth group informs you that he's going to a Catholic high school this year so he can take participate in their highly-regarded football program. He explains that he'll have to take doctrine classes and attend chapel there but that he can't see all that much difference between his new school and his old (Protestant) Christian school. How would you respond?

2. Visual: Catholic View of Salvation
Try this activity to provide a visual reminder of the way Catholics view salvation. Place a string across the room about three feet high. On one side of the string sprinkle a candy treat on the floor; on the other side, line up the group against the wall. The group has to get from one side to the other without going under or touching the string. They may not use chairs or any other furniture or equipment in the room. Give them some time to attempt it—most

will figure out some way to do it. Debrief with questions like these: **How did it feel to be on the wrong side of the barrier? How did you feel trying to get to the other side? How would you have felt if you couldn't get over to the other side? How would you have felt if I had cut the string down and simply let you walk across the room?**

Ask students to relate this exercise to the Catholic view of salvation versus the Protestant view. (The Catholic view requires believers to use their own efforts—get over the string—to reach the fully the reward of salvation; the Protestant view holds that salvation is first of all God's work, our own works don't help us reach the reward of eternal life. In effect, the string is down—there are no barriers to salvation that we have to overcome by our own actions.)

3. Field Trip

We suggest that you and your group attend worship at a Catholic Church if possible. You may want to consult *How to Be a Perfect Stranger* (see p. 12) to prepare your group for the experience. Review the diagram of the interior of a Catholic Church in the participant newspaper, and check "Getting Outside the Room" on pages 10-11. Be sure your group understands that only Catholics in good standing may participate in the Eucharist; your group will only be watching the Mass.

Afterwards, discuss the experience using questions like these:

- **What new or unusual experiences did you have? How did you feel about it?**

- **What senses were employed in worship? How did that affect your experience?**

- **Were there elements of this worship that you wish were part of our worship services? What elements of worship help you worship best? What did you think was the aim or theme of worship as it was communicated by the liturgy?**

4. Video Reminder

TRAVARCA offers nearly a dozen videos on various aspects of Catholicism. Check the list on pages 13-14 for details and ordering information.

If Group Members Are Adults or Young Adults

Step 1: You will probably not need to do the shoe game to get your group engaged in the session (but don't hesitate to try it if you'd like). Open with the group's experiences and knowledge of the Catholic Church. Some of your group may have been raised Catholic or attended Catholic schools or universities; others may have family who are Catholic or they may have attended Catholic weddings or funerals. You can also introduce the session by sharing whatever current news item is the focus of media attention on the Catholic Church. Chances are that something in the news is about the pope or the priesthood. Find a common starting place for your group before raising the issue of what questions they have about the Catholic tradition.

Step 2: Again, use the wisdom of your group's experiences to inform the content of the articles in the participant newspaper. What stories can someone in your group tell about an Irish ancestor's experience as an immigrant, for example? What do they know firsthand about worship in a Catholic Church?

Step 3: Spend some time reflecting on how praying to saints compares to the prayer chains we set up in our churches. Is there a difference between asking other Christians to pray for a relative who is facing chemo and asking Saint Jude to intercede on that person's behalf?

You may also want to raise this question: Has anyone ever called you a saint or have you ever expressed that thought about another believer? What do you think that means? Is it biblical?

Step 4: Questions of evaluation can be added to this discussion: How would you evaluate the list of what makes a "good Catholic"? What definition of discipleship do the lists assume? How would you compare them?

Step 5: For your closing prayer, ask the group to share the names of those whom they would describe as heroes of faith in their lives and then give thanks for them and their faithful witness.

The Lutheran Tradition

3

Scripture/Confession	Romans 1:17; Romans 5:1-2; Ephesians 2:8-9; Heidelberg Catechism, Q&A 61
Session Focus	The Lutheran Christian tradition is the first of all Protestant reform movements and subsequent North American denominations. The key faith distinctive of this tradition is a strong emphasis on the grace God extends to sinful humanity, providing full salvation and forgiveness through Jesus Christ.
Session Goals	• to understand the significant role the Lutheran tradition has played in church history • to identify the four key themes of Luther's theology • to appreciate the history of the Lutheran churches in North America • to say what it means to be "justified by faith" • to feel assured that we are loved by God and are recipients of God's grace
Key Distinctive of This Faith Tradition	The first Lutheran statement of faith and its most essential confession is a document written by one of Martin Luther's colleagues, Philipp Melanchthon, in 1531. Asked by the Holy Roman Emperor Charles V to prepare a statement that would explain the essential teachings of the Reformers to a group of German princes called to a meeting in the town of Augsburg, Melanchthon wrote the document that came to be called the *Augsburg Confession*. The emperor rejected the teachings of the Reformers, but the Confession lives on. At its heart is the great truth of salvation by grace alone:

> Our works cannot reconcile us to God or merit forgiveness of sins, grace, and justification, but that we obtain this only by faith when we believe that we are received into favor for Christ's sake, who alone has been set forth the Mediator and Propitiation, 1 Tim. 2, 5, in order that the Father may be reconciled through Him. Whoever, therefore, trusts that by works he merits grace, despises the merit and grace of Christ, and seeks a way to God without Christ, by human strength, although Christ has said of Himself: I am the Way, the Truth, and the Life. John 14, 6. This doctrine concerning faith is everywhere treated by Paul, Eph. 2, 8: By grace are ye saved through faith; and that not of your selves; it is the gift of God, not of works.

> —from section 20: Faith and Good Works

This became the battle cry of Luther and his followers. Grace is at its center: grace, the undeserved favor God extends to sinful humanity, providing salvation and forgiveness through Jesus Christ. Above all else, according to Lutherans, God is gracious. Talking about God means talking first of all about grace.

As followers of John Calvin, we also emphasize *sola gratia,* by grace alone. This teaching became one of the key truths of the Reformation. God's gift to the church through Luther was this emancipation of salvation from self-help piety and good works. But we Calvinists differ a bit when it comes to defining the essence of God. Yes, we say, God is about grace but God is also about sovereignty. Isn't the first thing we know about God not that God loves us but that God is our king? As almighty Ruler, God acts graciously and lovingly.

That might seem like a bit of theological hair splitting but it does create some differences in how Lutherans and Calvinists understand the aim of salvation. A Lutheran, for example, would agree with the Canons of Dort but would want to modify a few of its statements:

- Christ's atonement was unlimited, that is, for all people, not just for those who believe.
- Some people clearly can resist God's grace (the Bible shows us many who did so).
- It is possible for people to lose their faith if they do not live a life of repentance and faithfulness.

Underlying all those modifications is the Lutheran understanding of God's generous grace—God desires the salvation of all, not just some.

While we agree with this basic tenet, we do not arrive at all the same conclusions. Nevertheless, on the essentials we stand together: justification is by grace alone, received through faith alone. John Calvin called this "the main hinge on which religion turns."

Materials

Leader
- Bible
- Participant newspaper: The Lutheran Tradition
- Newsprint, marker
- Listing of local Lutheran churches from newspaper, yellow pages, or Internet
- Optional: student presentations (see end of session 2 for details)
- Optional: large poster of the Christian family tree (see session 1)

Key websites you may want to check for more information:
www.elca.org (Evangelical Lutheran Church in America)
www.elcic.org (Evangelical Lutheran Church in Canada)

Participants
- Bible
- Participant newspaper: The Lutheran Tradition
- Photocopy of Christian family tree (see session 1)
- Optional: one cookie for each participant. Cookies should be as uniform in appearance as possible; store-bought cookies like Chips Ahoy or Oreos are good.

Session at a Glance

Step 1: We use the Christian family tree to review the Western/Eastern split and to add new data (5 minutes).

Step 2: Using the student newspaper, we read and discuss articles about Martin Luther and his followers (15-20 minutes).

Step 3: We pair off and read articles about beliefs and worship to each other, focusing on grace as a key Lutheran distinctive (20 minutes).

Step 4: In this optional step, we look at any additional articles the group wants to discuss (5-15 minutes).

Step 5: We wrap up the session by taking a quick look at the four *sola* principles of Reformation Churches, then close by responsively reading Psalm 46 or a prayer written by Luther (10 minutes).

Note: We suggest a minimum of an hour for these sessions. You'll find that you can easily expand that time, even adding an extra session on each faith tradition, using the unread articles in the newspaper and the ideas in the course introduction. If you must cut the time to, say, forty-five minutes, you'll need to omit some of the activities we suggest and shorten others. **In this session, for example, you could omit the "choosing a leader" activity in step 2 and omit step 4.**

Step 1

Getting Started

Hand out copies of the family tree (see session 1 for details) and this session's newspaper. Quickly review the data you've entered so far: the date 1054, the split into the Eastern and Western branches, and the Roman Catholic branch we looked at last time. Then ask questions like these:

- **Why did the Eastern and Western branches split?**

- **What's unique about the left-handed branch?** (It's got lots of smaller branches; the right one doesn't.)

- **Why is that?** (Hopefully, someone will indicate that the numerous branches are the result of the Reformation or say something about Protestant churches.)

Explain that from now on we'll begin focusing on the left or Western branch of Christianity, beginning with the followers of Martin Luther, who began the movement called the Reformation. Ask them to write 1517 at the bottom of the first branch and then write "Protestant churches" along that branch. Write "Lutheran/Evangelical" on the first branch off from the Protestant Church branch. (If this sounds complicated, please see the diagram on p. 3 of the student newspaper.) If you've made a large copy of the family tree, use it (or your overhead) to show where the new data goes.

Write the words "Lutheran" and "Evangelical" on your board or newsprint and refer the group to the definitions of these terms in "Sound Bites."

Step 2

The Leader and His Followers

In this step we'll look at two articles in the student newspaper: "Here I Stand" (p. 4) and "Luther's Rose" (p. 1). If you asked students to present these articles, please see the option below.

Just for fun, ask your group to put their heads together and see how many facts they can come up about Martin Luther. (If you suspect your group knows little or nothing about Luther, omit this lead-in.) Let them give a few, then ask them to silently read "Here I Stand" (p. 4). As they read, ask them to underline or highlight a "lightbulb"—one fact they didn't know (or forgot) about Luther or something they found especially interesting. Review the results with them. You may want someone to read Romans 1:17 aloud to the group ("The righteous will live by faith . . .").

Then divide into groups of three to four students each. Say something like this: **I'm going to call out some qualifications. In your group, pick out a leader who meets those qualifications. The first group that figures out who its leader is, wins the round.** If your group is small, stay in one group and challenge the class to see how fast they can name someone who meets the qualification you mention.

47

Here are some leadership "qualifications" to mention:

first round: the person who has the longest hair
second round: the person who has the busiest schedule
third round: the person who has the shortest last name
fourth round: the person with the most money in his or her wallet or purse
fifth round: the person who is most likely to be a multimillionaire

Ask: **How does this exercise compare to the way that leaders are chosen in real life?** Note that Martin Luther had no aim to be the leader of what came to be called the Reformation when he nailed his debate theses to the church door of Wittenberg. **What qualities made Luther a leader?** (A conviction that he was right; the ability to be a good spokesperson; having vision—the ability to see what no one else could see; a calling from God.)

Raise the question of what happened after Luther got the Reform movement started. **How did Luther's followers become Lutherans or Evangelicals?** Have everyone silently read the article "Luther's Rose." Then quickly review "Facts and Figures" and allow for any questions. Note which Lutheran churches are in your community and whether any are "the church down the street."

Option: Kids as Teachers

If you found two volunteers to read the above articles at home and summarize them for the class, substitute their reports for the silent reading described above. The first report should review the life and importance of Luther. The second should highlight Lutheran history in North America. Be sure to allow time for questions from the group after each summary.

Step 3

Belief and Worship

Direct the group to the two articles on belief and worship: "What This Church Believes" (p. 2) and "Worship: The Means of Grace" (p. 3). Have them take turns reading the articles aloud to each other, in pairs, with the person who's not reading circling the word "grace" every time it appears in the text.

After ten minutes, or sooner if students are finished, ask:

- **How many times did "grace" appear in the text?** (About eighteen.)

- **So what must be the key idea in this Christian tradition?** (Grace!)

- **Why is grace the heart of Lutheran teaching?** (It was the break-through idea that led Luther to salvation; salvation is a result of God's grace to us.)

- **What is grace?** Solicit some definitions. You may want to have someone read aloud the paragraph on page 2 that begins: "If you could condense all of Lutheran teaching into one word . . ."

- **How is grace at the center of Lutheran worship?** (In the preaching of the gospel and through the sacraments—note the Lutheran understanding of baptism and the Lord's Supper and how their idea is different from the Reformed understanding.)

- **What difference does it makes that salvation is through grace alone?**

Option: Grace Cookies

Take out the cookies you have brought to class, one per person. (Remember, these should be uniform cookies that look as much alike as possible.) Pass around the plate of cookies and have everyone select a cookie. If you wish, serve some juice or pop with the cookie.

As kids are enjoying the cookies, ask:

- **Why did you choose the cookie you just ate? Because of its size, shape, or something else?**

- **Did your cookie deserve to be chosen on the basis of its distinctiveness? Was there anything about the cookie that singled it out as being worthy of selection?**

- **How is your choice of a cookie like grace?** (In the words of Cookie Monster: "I love cookie; I eat cookie.") Ask again what grace is. (The unmerited, undeserved love God freely extends to us without our knowledge or consent).

Step 4

Optional

As time permits, refer to any additional articles you or the kids want to talk about.

- If you're a Lake Wobegon fan, now is the time to play your favorite story from *Gospel Birds* or other Keillor recordings (see "Want to Read More?" p. 4).

- If the church down the street is Lutheran or a Lutheran cousin, find it in "Facts and Figures" (p. 1) or "Lutheran Cousins" (p. 3). Supplement with information you've gathered about this particular church (for example, distribute copies of their bulletin or belief statements).

- Explore how Christians differ on the number of books in the Bible ("How Many Books in the Bible?") or on the order of the commandments ("Which Commandment Was That?"). Both articles are on page 4.

Step 5

Four Sola Principles

Write *sola scriptura, sola fides, sola gratia,* and *sola Christus* on newsprint or on your board. Ask for guesses on what *sola* might mean (alone—think of a solo sung in church). See if the group can say what each of the four terms means. Summarize by reading the definitions from "Sound Bites" on page 2.

- *sola scriptura, sola fides, sola gratia, sola Christus:* the four great principles of the Reformation (Scripture alone, faith alone, grace alone, Christ alone). The Bible is the highest authority for faith, justification is only attained through faith; redemption comes through God's grace and choice; Christ alone is the one through whom we can approach God.

Point out that these four great principles are held by the Reformed/Presbyterian tradition as well as by the Lutheran tradition.

49

Read Ephesians 2:8-9 together in unison. Ask if students understand what it means that we are justified (made right with God) "by grace, through faith." Affirm the great love God has for each member of the group and remind them that each is a recipient of God's grace.

You could close your session by reading Psalm 46 responsively (it's the basis for Luther's great hymn "A Mighty Fortress Is Our God"). Or, if you prefer, pray the morning prayer by Luther (see "Pause Button," p. 4).

Option: More on Grace

You can extend your discussion of justification by reading Romans 5:1-2 and Q&A 61 of the Heidelberg Catechism:

Q. Why do you say that
by faith alone
you are right with God?

A. It is not because of any value my faith has
that God is pleased with me.
Only Christ's satisfaction, righteousness, and holiness
make me right with God.
And I can receive this righteousness and make it mine
in no other way than
by faith alone.

Looking Ahead to the Next Session

Read the newspaper on the Presbyterian and Reformed tradition, paying special attention to the denominations in this tradition that you are least familiar with. You may want to do some further reading on them.

You will need to take a little extra time to make some "clue cards" for a scavenger game (see step 1) and a dozen question cards (see step 2). Both can be made from notecards.

You will be connecting the history of this tradition to your own particular congregation and denomination. Be sure you know how and when and where your denomination and congregation got started. Consider bringing in your local church "historian" to tell (in five minutes or less!) the story of how your congregation started.

Check out your denomination's website and see if there are resources you could use in the session (see listing of websites in the participant newspaper). You may want to use a video presentation prepared by your denomination about your church's history or current life together.

Reformed: What It Means, Why It Matters by Robert DeMoor is a very useful booklet that offers a brief history of the Reformed tradition and several "distinctives" of its theology in four, easy-to-read chapters. It's available from Faith Alive Christian Resources.

Consider doing two sessions on the Reformed/Presbyterian tradition: one on the general tradition and a second on your particular denomination. Look at "Extending the Session" in session 4 for ideas on how this could be done.

Extending the Session

1. The Ninety-five Theses

At the beginning of the session, distribute small pieces of paper—about ¼ of a page in size. As the group discusses and reads the material, have them use fine-tipped markers to write down the sentences they think could have been one of the ninety-five theses (debatable statements relating to belief or practice) Luther posted on the door of the Wittenberg Church (see "Here I Stand," p. 4). Remind them to do this throughout the session, especially just after you've finished an article. At the end of the session, tape these on the door of your room and see if you have ninety-five! If possible, leave the statements posted until next time, when you can use them to review the Lutheran tradition.

2. A Mighty Fortress

Distribute hymnals containing Luther's Reformation hymn, "A Mighty Fortress Is Our God." If you have a recording of this song, play it for the group. Have the group underline or note two or three specific lines that relate to Luther's struggles to reform the church. Do the same for lines that show Luther's personal hope and strength. Finally, discuss why this song is still so appealing to so many Christians today.

3. Luther Quotes

Pick one of the following statements of Martin Luther and tell how it applies to your Christian understanding of faith and life.

- "How we are saved is the chief of the whole Christian doctrine. . . . God has declared no article so plainly and openly as this, that we are saved only by Christ."

- "When I consider my crosses, tribulations and temptations, I shame myself almost to death, thinking what they are in comparison to the sufferings of my blessed Savior, Christ Jesus."

- "None can believe how powerful prayer is, and what it is able to effect, but those who have learned it by experience. It is a great matter, when in extreme need, to take hold on prayer. I know whenever I have earnestly prayed, I have been amply heard and have obtained more than I prayed for; God, indeed, sometimes delayed, but at last he came."

4. Reminders: Field Trip, Guest Speaker, Video

Lutheran worship services are sufficiently different from those in the Reformed/Presbyterian tradition to make attending a Lutheran service an attractive option for your group. See "How to Visit Another Christian Church" (p. 12) for helpful tips and suggestions. Ask your group to be especially watchful for how grace is evident.

Asking a Lutheran to visit your class is another option (contact the pastor of a neighboring church for suggestions). See "Hosting a Guest from Another Christian Tradition" (p. 11) for general suggestions and procedures.

Finally, check out the half-dozen videos that TRAVARCA offers on the Lutheran tradition (see p. 14 for details and ordering information).

If Group Members Are Adults or Young Adults

Step 1: Ascertain who in the group has prior experience or firsthand knowledge of the Lutheran tradition. Use this person as a resource throughout the session.

Step 2: You may want to omit the "choosing a leader" activity. If you do decide to use it, adapt it to the traits of your group: the person who drives the oldest car, the person who has the most children, and so on.

Step 3: Have adults read the articles aloud or silently, rather than to each other. Also, make up your own (more challenging) questions on the newspaper articles. Use the wisdom of your group's experiences to inform the content of these articles. You may also want to expand on the discussion of grace as your group indicates interest. You could add questions about "cheap grace" or why we find it hard to accept that salvation is solely the work of God.

Comparing the history of Lutheran churches and communities in North America to that of Dutch, Reformed communities might be interesting. You could also explore how Luther and Calvin arrived at such different answers to the question of how a Protestant church worships.

Step 4 (optional): You'll want to base your selection of additional readings on the group's interests. A group that's fairly knowledgeable about church history may want to explore the key role Luther played in defining Western Christianity. Have them react to the statement "All Christian traditions that follow Luther have to take him into account." In what ways is this true?

Step 5: Consider using activity 2 ("A Mighty Fortress") under the heading "Extending the Session." Your group may want to close by singing the song together.

The Presbyterian and Reformed Tradition

4

Scripture/Confessions

Psalm 24:1; 1 Corinthians 10:31; Heidelberg Catechism, Q&A 1; *Our World Belongs to God: A Contemporary Testimony,* stanzas 1, 2, 6, 45; Westminster Confession of Faith, Chapter II; Shorter Catechism, Q&A 1, 100-107

Session Focus

Churches that embrace the teachings of John Calvin call themselves Reformed, an historical definition meaning a Reformation church, a church that is Presbyterian in its system of government, and a church that is Calvinistic in its theological distinctiveness. The key faith distinctives of Calvinism are an emphasis on the sovereignty of God and the lordship of Christ over every area of life.

Session Goals

- to understand the terms *Reformed, Presbyterian, Congregational,* and *Calvinist*
- to appreciate the four kinds of Reformed churches that contributed to the settling of North America and to locate our own congregation within the Reformed tradition
- to identify the proclamation of the Word as the focus of Reformed worship
- to describe what's meant by the sovereignty of God (a key Reformed emphasis) and the lordship of Christ over every area of life.
- to mention one way that this world and life view makes a difference in our lives

Key Distinctive of This Faith Tradition

If grace is the key to the Lutheran tradition, then *sovereignty* is the magic word that opens the Reformed tradition. The Reformed emphasis on the sovereignty of God and the lordship of Christ over all of life is a key theological legacy to the Christian faith.

The doctrine of the sovereignty of God is not exclusive to Reformed churches, of course, but it is an emphasis on which we build our theology. "God is in control. God does for us what we cannot do for ourselves," says Bob DeMoor in *Reformed: What It Means, Why It Matters.* "If God had not chosen us first, we would never have chosen him. If God did not give us saving faith through the Holy Spirit and his Word, we would never be able to conjure up that faith in and of ourselves. . . . Because God is in control over everything, I can be sure I'm right with him—not because I'm good enough or strong enough. If we belong to God, nothing . . . can snatch us from our Savior's grip" (p. 24).

God owns this world and in Jesus Christ is reclaiming it and restoring it to its original purpose and glory. And so, say Reformed Christians, our task is to share in that work of reclamation. In all of our living—our work, our leisure, our politics, our finances, our parenting, our stewardship—we seek to transform and restore our world. This shapes the Calvinistic "world and life view."

Out of these two principles—sovereignty and Jesus' lordship—have arisen many contributions to North American culture, history, and society. As you read through the participant newspaper, you can't help but be impressed by the gifts the churches of this tradition have given to our systems of government, law codes, standard of living, and quality of life. What's listed is really

Key

This focus/belief is evidenced in the early work of the Reformed in the US.

only the tip of an iceberg. Church historian Mark Noll claims that no one can understand the history and culture of North America without taking into account the story of the Presbyterian and Reformed churches. While not the largest group of Protestants in the continent, they were the single most powerful. Called by their Sovereign to extend the kingdom of God through every occupation and type of work, our predecessors took their vocations seriously. Our North American heritage is profoundly shaped by their actions.

Among the gifts that arise from the diversity within our tradition are the inclusivity of the United Church of Christ, the leadership of the Presbyterian Church (USA) in addressing social evils, the doctrinal and confessional integrity of the Reformed branches, and the high regard for Scripture of our Korean congregations. While we maintain distinctions among us, together we share a rich theological heritage shaped by a regard for stable and orderly church government, a focus on the importance of God's Word accompanied by a deep appreciation for its study and scholarship, and a heartfelt desire to live our theology.

Our tradition is being challenged to live up to the name Reformed. Observers of current trends and soothsayers predicting the future of Christianity note that the tradition is declining in numbers and losing its dominance in key areas of leadership. What changes are our always-reforming churches being asked to make? Do traditional labels such as Reformed and Presbyterian still communicate with our culture? How will we continue to honor our calling to extend God's kingdom into a new millennium?

Many answers have been suggested. But the solution really lies in the hands of the members of your group. As you lead your teens today, remind yourself that you are nurturing the next generation of our tradition's leadership. Celebrate with them who we have been and who we are, and encourage them to meet the challenge of defining who we will be.

Materials	**Leader**

Leader
- Bible
- Participant newspaper: The Presbyterian and Reformed Tradition
- Newsprint, marker
- Listing of local Reformed and Presbyterian churches from newspaper, yellow pages, or Internet
- Clues for the scavenger hunt, written on notecards and hidden before the session begins (see step 1)
- Questions on notecards, one question per card (step 1)
- "Agree or Disagree" quiz (p. 3), one copy per group member
- Optional: denominational video explaining its history and tradition (such as the 17-minute *Who Are We Presbyterians?* by the Presbyterian Church [USA] or parts of the 110-minute video *Our Family Album—the Drama* by the Christian Reformed Church, suggested for mature classes who want to spend an extra session viewing the video)
- Optional: large poster of Christian family tree (see session 1)
- Optional: copies of key doctrinal or confessional statement of your denomination (Westminster Confession, Heidelberg Catechism, or Brief Statement of Faith of the Presbyterian Church [USA]; step 5)

Key websites you may want to check for more information:
www.crcna.org (Christian Reformed Church in North America)
www.pcanet.org (Presbyterian Church in America)
www.pcusa.org (Presbyterian Church USA)
www.rca.org (Reformed Church in America)
www.epc.org (Evangelical Presbyterian Church)

Participants
- Participant newspaper: The Presbyterian and Reformed Tradition
- Copy of Christian family tree (see session 1)
- "Agree or Disagree" quiz (p. 63), one copy per group member

Session at a Glance	*Step 1:* We have a scavenger hunt to search for clues that identify our topic of study today (10 minutes).

Step 2: Using questions on notecards as guides, we read four articles covering the history and influence of churches in the Presbyterian and Reformed tradition. We place our denomination on the Christian family tree (20 minutes).

Step 3: We use "Sound Bites" to look at some basic definitions, then use "What This Church Believes" to see how the concept of God's sovereignty drives much of Reformed theology (10-15 minutes).

Step 4: We see that worship in the Reformed tradition is Word-centered (10 minutes).

Step 5: We take and discuss an agree/disagree quiz that applies the teachings about God's sovereignty and our world and life view to our daily lives (10 minutes).

Note: We suggest a minimum of an hour for these sessions. You'll find that you can easily expand that time, even adding an extra session on each faith tradition, using the unread articles in the newspaper and the ideas in the course introduction. If you must cut the time to, say, forty-five minutes, you'll need to omit some of the activities we suggest and shorten others. **In this session, for example, you could omit step 1 and use the option for step 2 (or omit an article).**

Step 1	**Getting Started**

Write each of the six clues (below) on an index card or piece of paper. Each card will direct participants to the next clue. The first clue should direct them to a point outside the room, then lead them on a tour of your church, and finally end up at your church sign or door. These are suggested clues; you'll want to adapt them to fit your church:

Clue 1 (handed out in the classroom): The faith tradition we are studying today practices infant baptism.

Clue 2 (located at the baptismal font): Likes to sing in worship.

Clue 3 (located at the organ, piano, or music director's stand): Emphasizes the central place of Scripture as the authority for faith and life.

Clue 4 (hidden at the pulpit): Governed by a consistory/session/council.

Clue 5 (hidden in the council meeting room): Values education and learning.

Clue 6 (hidden in church library): Tells all who approach what kind of church it is.

(Final stop is the church sign/door, assuming there's some indication there that the church is Reformed or Presbyterian. If there's no sign, we suggest you make one and hang it on the church door!)

Meet your group there and ask if they've figured out which Christian tradition we're discussing today. Affirm that it is the Presbyterian and Reformed tradition.

Note: If your group has fewer than ten participants, have the whole group locate the clues together. If your group is really large, break into teams and start them off at different times. Or change the clues and do more of the hunt outside the building, adding clues that take them to the portrait wall of your past pastors, the pastor's study, and so on. Another way to hide the clues is to give them to people who are in on the game and position themselves by the answer site.

Option: Timesaver

If your time is very limited or if the above "church tour" just isn't practical for you, just use the clues as a guessing game. Kids should hold off their answers until you've given all the clues. Or go directly to step 2.

Step 2

Questions About History and Influence

As the group comes back into the room, hand out notecards on which you've written the following questions, one to a card. These questions are based on the articles "A New Faith Tradition and a Young Continent" (p. 1), "Facts and Figures" (p. 1), "Timeline" (p. 3), and "Know Any of These People?" (p. 4).

1. What did John Calvin do that made him a leader of the Reformation? Mention three things. *Wrote the Institutes, lead Geneva, taught.*
2. What two words apply to the churches founded by John Calvin? What do these words mean? *Reformed, Calvinistic*
3. What four major Reformed groups settled in North America? Where did they settle? *French Huguenots, Puritans, Dutch Reformed, S/I Pres.*
4. From which of the four major Reformed groups did our denomination eventually come? *S/I Pres.*
5. In what three ways did Reformed people have a strong influence on the early history of the United States? *Colleges, leaders in Ref churches, influential ministers*
6. Name three famous Reformed/Presbyterian people. What are they famous for? *John Witherspoon, Emily Dickinson, James Madison*
7. What are some issues that split up churches in the Reformed/Presbyterian tradition? What examples of reconciliation/unity can you find?
8. How many denominations are from the Reformed/Presbyterian tradition? *23* Mention two you didn't previously know were in this group.
9. What happened in the nineteenth century that greatly increased the number of churches in the Reformed tradition? *New wave of immigrants,*
10. ~~What will (should) Reformed churches always be marked by?~~
11. What are three new facts or ideas you learned from reading thee articles?
12. When did your denomination first come to North America? Where? *1973*

Distribute the notecards, giving each person at least one card. If you have more than a dozen students, give duplicates of question 11. If you have fewer than a dozen, give more than one card to a student.

Then proceed in *one* of the two ways suggested here:

A. Have students take turns reading the articles out loud. When someone hears what could be an answer to the question on his or her notecard, he or she says (loudly!) "Question! Question!" The student then reads the question from the notecard and either answers it himself or chooses another student to answer it.

B. Students read the articles silently, watching for an answer to the question on their notecard(s). After ten minutes or so, everyone gets a chance to answer his or her question. Take the questions in sequence, as given above. Consider pairing weaker readers with good readers; let them work on their assigned questions together.

Use question 12 as a lead-in to adding the Christian family tree. Distribute the family trees to their owners and let them fill in the Reformed branch (see newspaper, p. 2). If you're using a large family tree poster, have someone add the Reformed branch to it as well.

Take a moment to review the birthdate and birthplace of your own denomination, along with a few details of your choice. You may want to show students the details of the Reformed branch, perhaps even providing a diagram on chalkboard or newsprint. Here's a sample diagram for the Reformed Church in America or the Christian Reformed Church in North America:

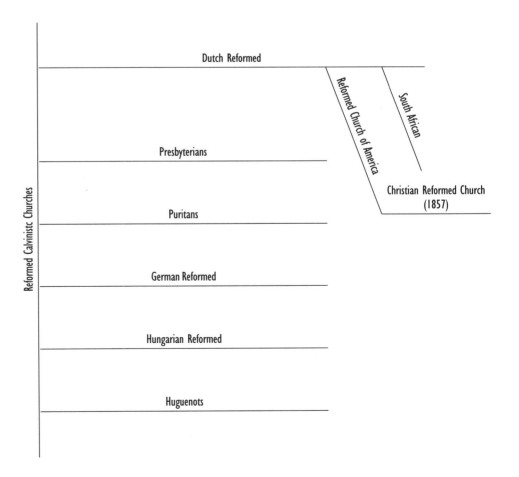

Option: Alternate Use of Questions

If you prefer, you could put the questions on a handout, leaving room for answers. Then divide up the questions equally among small groups. Have groups report on the answers to their assigned questions. Or simply use the questions (duplicated for students) to guide your discussion.

Option: Our Denomination

Concentrate the history part of this session on your denomination's own particular history using a denominational video, if available. Draw on the articles for helpful background and context. Or consider offering a second session on your denomination's and congregation's history. See "Extending the Session" on page 60.

Step 3

Basic Beliefs

Write these words on newsprint or on your board:

- Presbyterian
- Reformed
- Congregational
- Puritan

Ask someone to read—in random order—the definitions only of these words from "Sound Bites" on page 2; the others should match the definition to the word.

Then write the word *Calvinist* on the board and explain that all churches in this tradition are categories of the larger description we call Calvinist.

Ask, **What does it mean to be a *Calvinistic* church? What, despite all these different names and histories, do these churches have in common?**

To answer this question, have volunteers take turns reading the article "What This Church Believes." You will want to take a minute or two to be sure the group understands what *sovereignty* means, and that they know it is the basic idea from which flows most of Reformed theology. Then read through the remaining definitions.

Ask the group if they learned something about Reformed theology that they didn't know before or had forgotten. Give them a chance to ask any additional questions they may have about Calvinism.

Option: Personal Statements

If you have time, add the following to the above step. Prepare a handout on which you have written two incomplete sentences: "I am a Calvinist because . . ." and "I am a Christian because. . . ." Invite group members to (individually) complete the statements. Keep this on a voluntary basis, since you do not want to compel people to make statements they're not ready to make. After a few minutes, invite (but don't force) sharing of responses.

Step 4	## Reformed Worship

Remind your group of the clues of the hunt that took them into the sanctuary. Then ask questions like these:

Name some things we do in worship.

- **Based on those clues, what can we conclude about worship in the Reformed tradition?** (We baptize infants, participate in the Lord's Supper, sing, listen to sermons).

- **What clues do you have that the Word of God and the preaching of the Word are central to our worship?** (Note the position of the pulpit, placement of open Bible on the pulpit, and any other indicators.)

Have group members read the brief article "Worship: Centered on the Word." Continue by asking:

- **Honestly now, how do you feel about the sermon being the focus of Reformed worship?** (If you get complaints about the length of sermons, regale them with stories of the sermons you endured as a kid or the two separate hour-long sermons of the early Congregational churches. You should, however, help them understand what a gift a good sermon is as it conveys God's Word for our lives. Perhaps you can share how a sermon spurred your spiritual growth at a particular time.)

Conclude with this quote from the worship article: "Reformed worship is always focused on God, centered on the Bible, and connected to our world."

Option: More on Worship

Worship is a topic many teens enjoy discussing. Here are some additional questions and activities that you could explore if you have extra time:

Consider as we enter worship.

- If your group meets just after or before a worship service, ask how the worship service was "focused on God, centered on the Bible, and connected to our world." Refer to bulletins and the order of worship. You could also ask your group to apply the three criteria to an upcoming worship service.

- Have kids complete the statement "Worship in our congregation is most meaningful to me when . . ." or "If I could change one thing about the worship services in my church, it would be. . . ."

Step 5	## Wrap-up

Tell the group you'd like to think with them a bit more about the sovereignty of God. Say something along these lines: **If God is King of the entire world and everything in it is God's, what does that mean for us when it comes time to choose an occupation? Does it mean that our work can be a way to worship God? Are there some parts of our lives—say, for example, something as routine as doing our homework—that God really isn't much interested in, or that are "off limits" to God? Can we draw a line between holy stuff and ordinary stuff in our lives?**

Then distribute photocopies of the "Agree or Disagree" quiz (p. 63) and give the group two or three minutes to complete it. Review the statements with the group, highlighting and clarifying any misunderstandings about a Reformed world and life view. Explain that one very important way we understand the world is by seeing it through God's eyes. This means that we view the world as God does—everything in it is part of the kingdom of God and we are to be part of making that kingdom come. That Reformed world and life view is a major contribution to Christianity.

Ask each person to suggest one way that their world and life view makes a difference in their lives. (Use the quiz to help them think of something if they struggle with this.) Allow a minute for reflection, then go around the circle and share responses (students may say "pass" if they don't want to share).

Close by asking group members to pray silently for God's help in turning over an area of their lives to God that they are sometimes tempted to claim for themselves. You could close the prayer by asking everyone to read in unison the prayer from "Pause Button" on page 4.

As usual, encourage group members to read the rest of the newspaper at home this week. Point out some (unread) articles you think might be interesting to them.

Option: Alternate Closing

If you have time, close by reading in unison a small part of a confession or creed of your church that highlights the sovereignty of God and the lordship of Christ over all of life. For example, Heidelberg Catechism, Q&A 1, or *Our World Belong Belongs to God,* stanzas 1, 2, 6, 45 (both can be found at the back of the *Psalter Hymnal);* Shorter Catechism, Q&A 1, 26, 46, 101-103.

Looking Ahead to the Next Session

Review the newspaper on the Episcopalian/Anglican tradition and read the session plan. Decide which articles in the paper and which steps in the session you'll use with your group. Note any questions you have or further reading you will want to do.

As part of session 5, we suggest that you create a worship setting. Be sure to check the session plan early in the week as you consider what materials you'll need to gather ahead of time. In addition, we've got you making a "bridge" puzzle (don't worry, it's no big deal) and creating your own version of a three-legged stool. You even get to hand out candy at the end. All this makes for a very lively, hands-on session—with just a little extra prep work from you.

Extending the Session

1. Your Denomination and Congregation
You may want to take two sessions for this faith tradition. If so, use the first session to discuss the tradition in general, pretty much following today's session plan. Use the second session to focus more specifically on your own denomination and congregation.

For the second session, have your group research the sources you use (whether print, electronic, or media) to answer these questions about your denomination:

- **How does it relate to the Christian family tree?**
- **When and where did the founders of our denomination arrive in North America? Why did they come?**
- **When and why did our denomination separate from its mother church? What's the meaning of its name?**
- **Who were the early leaders of our denomination? What did they do?**

- **What were some of the special situations/difficulties God led our denomination through?**
- **What is the current size of our denomination? Where are its headquarters located?**
- **What are the special strengths or contributions of our denomination?**

Use additional local sources like your church historian to answer these questions about your congregation:

- **What is the founding date of our congregation?**
- **How and why was it founded?**
- **Where did it first meet? What was its size? What was its name? Who was its first minister?**
- **What are some significant stories of God's care of our congregation?**
- **What are some important struggles of our congregation?**
- **What are some significant changes that have taken place?**
- **Where does the church meet now? What is its current size? Who is the pastor(s)? What does its name mean?**

Another way to develop an additional session would be to set up stations organized around topics like origins, interesting people, hot issues, stats, and ministry. Each station could contain some materials for learning and a set of directions that outline an activity. Have group members circulate among the centers as they are available until they have visited all of them. You could also prepare a worksheet of questions that could be answered through visiting the stations. You may also want to bring in additional adult leaders from your congregation to host each station and answer the participants' questions.

2. Famous Calvinist Visit
Ask someone in your congregation to pose (complete with costume) as a significant person in the tradition's history—someone like John Calvin (remember that he was French!), Jonathan Edwards, or Harriet Beecher Stowe.

3. Who Leads This Church?
If you have extra time or are taking an extra session, be sure to discuss this article. The Presbyterian form of church government is a unique contribution of Calvinism. You could make the article more interesting to kids by having an elder and deacon and pastor visit your group and briefly explain their roles.

4. Guests, Videos
- Ask a pastor or educator from another denomination in the Reformed/Presbyterian tradition to visit the class. Talk together about how your denominations are similar yet different. See "Hosting a Guest from Another Christian Tradition" on page 11 for general suggestions and procedures.

- If a nearby congregation of your denomination has an ethnic background different from your own, ask a representational group (including teens) to meet with your group and share what it means to be a Reformed Christian, or have your group attend their worship. You'll find much to appreciate, even if the worship is conducted in a language other than what you are accustomed to.

- Check out over a dozen videos on the Reformed/Presbyterian tradition from TRAVARCA (see p. 14 for details and ordering information).

If Group Members Are Adults or Young Adults

Adjust your leadership depending on the age and membership longevity of your adults (lifelong members of your denomination or new members?). Focus on what will be new information for your group; don't only review prior knowledge. If you have new *and* experienced members in your group, you may want to have a private word with the experienced members of your group to explain that the session will focus on what the newer members need to learn about our tradition. Encourage them to see this session as a time to welcome and enfold relative newcomers.

A great resource for new members (and a good reminder for experienced members too) is Bob DeMoor's booklet *Reformed: What It Means, Why It Matters,* available from Faith Alive Christian Resources (www.faithaliveresources.org or 1-800-333-8300). In four interesting and easy-to-read chapters, DeMoor describes the history and doctrinal distinctives of the Reformed tradition.

Step 1: Don't hesitate to have the group get on its feet and do some running around, but using the clues as a guessing game may be more appropriate for adults. Depending on your group's knowledge, make the clues a bit more challenging and sophisticated.

Step 2: Rather than hand out questions on notecards, you could simply list all the questions on a handout and use them as a guide for discussing the articles. Adults or young adults may be quite interested in the history of your denomination. Help them see where your denomination "fits" in the spectrum within our tradition.

Steps 3-4: Your group may not need to use the "Sound Bites" definitions, but point them out as a reference. The ideas in "What This Church Believes" are worth discussing one point at a time. You may also want to use the following quote to further discuss the main ideas of Reformed theology: "The gospel is not a doctrine of the tongue, but of life. . . . Our religion will be unprofitable if it does not change our hearts, pervade our manners, and transform us into new creatures" (John Calvin, *The Golden Booklet of the True Christian Life).* You may want to use these additional questions:

- **Would you agree that sovereignty is the foundational tenet of Calvinism?**
- **Can you make a case for the authority of Scripture? Predestination?**
- **What stereotypes continue to haunt North American Calvinists? Are they based on historical fact or misunderstanding?**
- **Liturgical scholars point out that the one unique addition Calvin made to the liturgy of the Christian church that has been universally adopted is the prayer for illumination before a sermon or Scripture reading. Why do you think this is an important part of our worship?**

Step 5: Instead of the quiz, have the group turn to Psalm 8. Read the psalm and discuss how it captures the themes of God's sovereignty and the lordship of Christ over all of life. Close with a responsive prayer: after each member of the group offers a thanksgiving, the group responds with "O Lord, how majestic is your name in all the earth!"

Agree or Disagree?

Read the two Scripture passages and the ten statements that follow. For each statement, write "Agree" or "Disagree." Keep in mind what you've learned about what it means to be Reformed or Presbyterian as you answer.

The earth is the LORD's and everything in it,
the world and all who live in it.

—Psalm 24:1

So whether you eat or drink or whatever you do, do it all for the glory of God.

—1 Corinthians 10:31

Agree/Disagree

_____ 1. Jesus and me—that's all that really matters. Having a personal relationship with Christ and knowing I'm saved is what Christianity is all about.

_____ 2. It's OK for Christians to participate in a peace march or picket an abortion clinic.

_____ 3. Keeping Sunday holy is the most important way a Christian can honor God.

_____ 4. Christians who are musicians in popular music can be good witnesses for Christ.

_____ 5. I can honor God at a soccer game or by playing the Sims.

_____ 6. God cares if I don't do well on my SATs.

_____ 7. It's OK for a Christian to make a cool million a year, live in a mansion, and own classic Jags.

_____ 8. No one should look down on any career choice I make since any job or occupation is a way to glorify God.

_____ 9. A Christian lawyer can do more good in this world than a Christian pizza delivery guy.

_____ 10. Between global warming and terrorist attacks, there's not much reason anymore to think the world is ever going to be a better place.

The Episcopal/ Anglican Tradition

5

Scripture/Confession	Romans 12:1-2; Ephesians 5:19; Psalm 50:1-6; *Our World Belongs to God: A Contemporary Testimony,* stanza 39
Session Focus	The Episcopalian/Anglican churches are a "bridge" tradition between the Roman Catholic and Protestant faith traditions. The key faith distinctive of this tradition is an emphasis on a rich worship that fully engages our minds, hearts, and bodies.
Session Goals	• to understand the Episcopal/Anglican tradition as a "bridge" between Roman Catholic and Protestant churches • to describe the three-legged stool of Episcopal/Anglican theology • to experience elements of an Episcopal/Anglican worship service and to appreciate the relationship between worship and belief (a theology of worship) • to gain a sense of awe and wonder about God from the rich nature of Episcopal/Anglican worship
Key Distinctive of This Faith Tradition	If you asked a member of the Episcopal/Anglican tradition to describe her church, she might tell you that it's a Protestant church with a Roman Catholic heritage. Another member might tell you that it's really the Roman Catholic Church with a Protestant heritage. Who's right? Both are. The Episcopal or Anglican Church is a bridge between these two traditions. When Elizabeth I assumed the throne of England, the religious life of her country was in chaos. A national church that had separated from the Catholic Church over politics, not theology, was unique to the Reformation. Elizabeth's two predecessors, half brother Edward and half sister Mary, had taken two entirely different approaches to defining the English church. Their legacy was a country torn apart by violent, opposing theological loyalties. Elizabeth's solution was to take the best of both and blend them into something new: a church that continued the familiar liturgy of the Catholic Church but that embraced the theology of the Reformed Church. Informed by that Reformed viewpoint, the liturgical worship of the Anglican Church is focused on the Word of God. That Word is proclaimed in its prayers, songs, lectionary readings, and sermons; it is experienced in the sacrament of the Eucharist. To worship in an Episcopal Church is to feed on the Word of God in many different ways. Kneeling, singing, chanting, candles, choirs, rich vestments, and cathedral ceilings all reflect a "sensual theology." We worship God not just in our hearts, but with our voices, our sense of smell, our delight in beauty, our appreciation of a well-turned phrase, and our bended knees. God created every part of us for praise and we bring all those parts to worship each Sunday.

- God is a God of excellence, so we bring our best music and richest clothes.
- God is a God of wonder, so we come prepared to be awed and amazed at God's glory and magnificence.
- God is a God of power, so we come to kneel and bow down before our King.
- God is a God of sacrifice, so we come to celebrate a feast of thanksgiving for the greatest sacrifice of all.

When Reformed Christians attend an Episcopal service, it's easy to want to strip away the "nonessentials" and get down to the "main point" of the worship. With one hand we desperately search through the prayer book, trying to find the page from which the priest is reading, with the other hand we juggle the hymnal. We keep a sharp eye peeled on those who look like they know what they're doing so that we aren't standing when it's time to sit or sitting when it's time to kneel. We wonder why they can't just make the whole thing less complicated.

Still, the Anglican emphasis on physical acts of worship reminds us that our worship is enriched when not only our minds and hearts but also our bodies are engaged in praise; it is enhanced when we need to focus on a demanding liturgy; it is deepened when it borrows language from the hearts of those who have gone before us.

Memory Work

Leader
- Bible
- Participant newspaper: The Episcopal/Anglican Tradition
- Newsprint, marker
- Listing of local Episcopal/Anglican churches from newspaper, yellow pages, Internet
- Handmade two-sided "bridge" puzzle (see step 1 for directions) or alternate of individual puzzles
- 4 cereal boxes (or books or other rectangles) of the same size; wrap in paper and/or label each one as follows: the Bible, Tradition, Reason, Belief
- A copy of the *Book of Common Prayer* or the lectionary (see your pastor for a copy). You can also access the liturgical items you'll need at www.io.com/~kellywp. Click on the calendar date that you'll be leading this session and it will give you the three Scripture lessons and the collect for the day.
- Worship items: Bible, candles, communion chalice and paten, tablecloth, stole, flowers, incense, and any others you wish to add (see newspaper worship article for ideas)
- Roll of assorted Lifesavers or other assorted flavor candy
- Optional: large poster of Christian family tree (see session 1)

Key websites you may want to check for more information:
www.anglicancommunion.org
www.episcopalian.org/pttw/
www.youngepiscopalian.org

Participants
- Bible
- Participant newspaper: The Episcopal/Anglican Tradition
- Photocopy of Christian family tree (see session 1)

Session at a Glance	*Step 1:* We receive pieces of a single, large "bridge" puzzle (or individual puzzles) that the leader has prepared prior to the session (1-2 minutes).

Step 1: We receive pieces of a single, large "bridge" puzzle (or individual puzzles) that the leader has prepared prior to the session (1-2 minutes).

Step 2: We read about the history of the Episcopal/Anglican tradition, jot down pertinent information on the reverse side of the puzzle pieces, then assemble the pieces into a bridge and discuss how the Episcopal Church bridged the gap between contrasting cultures and churches. We add the Church of England branch to the Christian family tree (20 minutes).

Step 3: Using the visual of a three-legged stool, we look at Episcopal/Anglican beliefs (10 minutes).

Step 4: We experience some of the elements of an Episcopal worship service (15-20 minutes).

Step 5: As a wrap-up activity, we think of different "flavors" of worship, compare Reformed worship to Episcopal/Anglican worship, look at Scripture to examine the purpose of worship, and use a "bidding prayer" to close the session (10 minutes).

Note: We suggest a minimum of an hour for these sessions. You'll find that you can easily expand that time, even adding an extra session on each faith tradition, using the unread articles in the newspaper and the ideas in the course introduction. If you must cut the time to, say, forty-five minutes, you'll need to omit some of the activities we suggest and shorten others. **In this session, for example, you could omit step 1, using the option for step 2 instead. Step 4 can be shortened by using selected worship activities; step 5 can be limited to looking at the biblical purpose of worship and the closing prayer.**

Step 1

Getting Started

Before today's session, prepare a puzzle for your group using a single sheet of posterboard. Glue a full-size photo of a bridge or a simple drawing of a bridge to the posterboard (see p. 74 for a sketch of a bridge that you can enlarge). Cut the posterboard into as many pieces as you have group members. Leave the reverse side of each piece blank. Distribute the pieces with the bridge side down and ask the group not to turn their pieces over.

An alternative, especially if your class is small, is to give each participant his or her own puzzle on an 8½ x 11 piece of paper cut into several pieces.

Step 2

Piecing Together Episcopal/Anglican History

Hand out the participant newspaper and have the group turn to the history article "An English Church for an American Continent" (p. 1). This is a fairly long article with a lot of detail, so you'll want to break up the reading with different readers and stop for questions at the end of each section. As they are reading, each person should write on his or her puzzle piece a person, event, significant problem, and/or issue that strikes them as one of the "pieces" that make up the history of the Episcopal/Anglican Church. (You may even wish to assign a certain number of group members to each section so that the "pieces" will be varied.)

Afterward, have people share what they wrote on their puzzle piece and why (if some left their piece blank, supply a few ideas, using the "Timeline" entries.

Have the group assemble their pieces and then flip the puzzle over to reveal the bridge.

If you used the alternate approach of giving group members their own complete 8½ x 11 puzzle, have them write on the reverse side of all of their puzzle pieces (or at least as many as possible). Then have each person share at least a couple of the ideas he or she wrote down. Conclude by flipping the pieces over and assembling to reveal the bridge.

Give one of your group a marker and ask the group how the Episcopal Church could be defined as a bridge.

What contrasting pairs does it connect? (Your group will likely first say that it connects the Roman Catholic and Protestant traditions. Help them also see that it connected Celtic and Roman Christianity, Old World and New World, English and American/Canadian cultures, church and state, tradition and creativity. If they're stumped, supply half of the contrasting pair: church and _____; Old World and _____. As these are mentioned, mark them on the opposite sides of the bridge.

If you are using the alternate approach of individual bridge puzzles, have the kids write these contrasts on their own puzzle (it's best to tape the puzzle pieces together before writing).

Look over the article "Facts and Figures," then share with the group any information you've gathered about local Episcopal/Anglican churches.

Give group members their copy of the Christian family tree and fill in the Episcopal/Anglican branch off the Church of England (see the diagram on p. 2 of the newspaper). If you've made a large poster of the family tree, ask one of your group members to bring it up to date.

Option: Timesaver

If you choose not to use the puzzle idea, omit step 1, read the article as described in step 2, and have participants use notecards to record significant events/people/issues of Episcopal/Anglican history, then share with the group. Introduce the bridge idea by drawing a bridge on a sheet of newsprint and having participants tell how the Episcopal/Anglican tradition served as a bridge. Jot the contrasting pairs on either side of the bridge.

Step 3

p. 2
3 legged stool

What This Church Believes

Have kids read this short article to themselves. Then toss the four boxes you've labeled (Bible, tradition, reason, beliefs) at four different students. Challenge them to arrange the boxes in the shape of a three-legged stool (the "belief" box becomes the seat of the stool, the three supporting boxes are arranged in a triangle to support it). Talk about—and demonstrate with the boxes—what happens when you try to balance your beliefs on just one or two of the boxes. Ask the group how the Episcopalians use the Bible, tradition, and reason to determine right belief.

Option: Case Study

If you have time, have the group use this "three legged" approach by using this case study.

A good friend comes to you with a question. His World Civilizations class has finished studying the Indian continent and the Hindu religion. When the class discussed reincarnation, almost everybody in the class said they believed it was probable. He's not so sure, but it does sound like a better idea than either ending up in a fire or floating on a cloud. He knows you're a Christian and wants to know what you believe.

What would you say and how would you ground it in Scripture, tradition, and reason? For a variation on this idea, ask a couple of outgoing students to role-play the case study.

Step 4	## Experiencing the Episcopal/Anglican Way of Worship

p.3

This step attempts to re-create a typical worship setting for this faith tradition. It will take a bit of preparation on your part, but allowing your group members to experience this setting will be far more memorable than just reading an article about it. If time does not allow you to do everything described in this step, try to select at least enough activities to give your group a taste of this style of worship.

Prior to the session, drape a small table with a cloth that reflects the color of the current season of the liturgical year. Set out a chalice and paten for the Eucharist (you may also want to include the elements of wine and wafers, which can be purchased at a Christian supply store). Place candles on each side of the table along with flowers and incense. If possible, set a cross on or behind the table and a lectern to one side. Light the candles and incense, dim the lights.

Ask someone to read the opening paragraph of "Worship: The Response of the Created to the Creator." Have the group look at the worship setting you have created in the room and describe what they see. Ask, "What elements of worship do you see that we don't use in our congregation?" (Note the explanation of the candles and flowers in the diagram of the interior of an Episcopal Church.)

While a member of the group continues to read "The Worship Service," break at the appropriate times to do the actions described:

- Lead the group in the day's collect (a prayer that "collects" the prayers of the people) as they kneel (see Materials section for where to locate the collect for the day). *179 , 230*

- Ask three volunteers to read one of today's Scripture lessons (if you're short of time, settle for one or an abridged version of all three). Each reader should begin the reading by saying, **A reading lesson from _____.** At the end, the reader should say, **This is the Word of the Lord.** The group responds: **Thanks be to God.** Make sure the group stands for the reading of the gospel. *972*   *Eli's death, Wisdom Parable*

- As a group, profess the Apostles' Creed and exchange the sign of peace. *p. 120*

- Point out the liturgical colors in your room when your group reviews that section of the article.

- Point out the sacramental elements. If you wish, demonstrate how Episcopalians take communion. (Refer to "How to Visit an Episcopal Church," p. 4.)

White – Christmas
Red – Pentecost Day Feast days
Violet – Advent + Lent
Crimson – Holy Wk.
Green – Epiphany after Pentecost
Black – Funerals + Good Friday

69

- If you have a copy of the *Book of Common Prayer,* let the group page through it and see its contents.

Close this step with some of these discussion questions (use only the last two if time is limited):

- **What sights, sounds, and smells would you notice in an Episcopal/Anglican service? How would they affect your understanding of worship?**

- **How would the liturgy affect your participation in worship?**

- **What does the "body language" tell you about how this tradition understands worship? Would you feel comfortable worshiping in an Episcopal/Anglican church? Why or why not?**

- **What elements of worship in the Episcopal/Anglican tradition would you like to see included in your church's worship?**

Option: Summary Questions

If time permits and you sense the group needs a summary of the session, ask these questions:

- **How is this church a "bridge" between two Christian traditions?**

- **What are the relationships between the Bible, tradition, and reason in Episcopal/Anglican theology?**

- **What is the theme of Episcopal worship?**

Step 5

Wrap-up

Ask the group to think of a faith tradition's worship as a flavor. Hand out the candy (Lifesavers have a nice variety of flavors and colors) and ask what flavor they think Episcopal/Anglican worship would be. Do all Christian traditions have a unique flavor? Let them do some creative associations to determine the flavor of Orthodox, Roman Catholic, Lutheran, and Reformed worship.

Discuss further, selecting from the questions below as time and the maturity of your group suggest:

- **What determines the flavor of someone's worship?** (Who they believe God is and what they believe worship is for.)

- **Based on what we've read and observed, what does Episcopal worship tell us about God?** (God is above us, God is our king, our creator, someone very different from us.)

- **What does it tell us about why we worship?** (We worship to praise God with all of who we are—body, heart, soul, and mind.)

You may want to read this Q&A from the catechism of the Episcopal Church:

Q. What is corporate worship?

A. In corporate worship, we unite ourselves with others to acknowledge the holiness of God, to hear God's Word, to offer prayer, and to celebrate the sacraments.

—From *The Book of Common Prayer*

- **Is Episcopal worship a totally different flavor than Reformed worship—like comparing apples to cranberries—or is it a slighter difference—like comparing cranberry juice to cranapple juice? Why do you think so?** (Both share the idea of humankind as creatures to Creator, as subjects to our King [sovereignty, remember?]. But the Reformed tradition places much less emphasis on the sensual aspects of worship. Perhaps your congregation embraces a more visual style of worship than Reformed worship of the past. You may want to highlight that both kinds of worship are about the Word but that in historical Reformed worship, the emphasis has been on the spoken and written Word, not the sacramental Word.)

- **Are all flavors of worship equally valid as long as they are the same kind of candy? Why do you think so?**

Have the group turn to Romans 12:1-2 and Ephesians 5:19. What do these texts seem to be telling us is the purpose of worship? You may also want to refer to *Our World Belongs to God: A Contemporary Testimony*, stanza 39:

Our new life in Christ
is celebrated and nourished
in the fellowship of congregations
where God's name is praised,
his Word proclaimed,
his Way taught;
where sins are confessed,
prayers and gifts are offered,
and sacraments are celebrated.

- **If it's true that the way we worship shapes what we believe, can we borrow worship flavors from other Christian traditions and still worship as Reformed Christians? How?**

If your group enjoys discussing this idea of flavors of worship, extend the discussion with additional questions like these:

- **If you could create the perfect flavor of worship, what would it be?**

- **How would God be honored by your flavor?**

Close the session with your choice of the following:

- Read Psalm 50:1-6 responsively as a prayer of praise.

- Teach your group the type of prayer often used by the Episcopal Church, the "bidding prayer." A leader begins by stating a topic that is to be prayed for—"bidding." For example: **That this day be holy, good, and peaceful . . . That our sins may be forgiven . . . That there may be peace**

and unity in our church and in the world . . . This is followed by a time of silent prayer or short prayers from the group. To conclude the prayer, the leader says, **Lord, in your mercy,** and the group responds, **Hear our prayer.** The length of the prayer is determined by the number of "bidding" statements.

- Remind your group of the sense of awe and wonder about God that Episcopal/Anglican worship inspires. Invite them to offer sentence prayers that express their own praise and wonder at our great God. A possible starter statement: **God, I praise you because . . .**

- As leader, say the prayer for young persons found in "Pause Button" (newspaper, p. 4).

Looking Ahead to the Next Session	Review the newspaper "Radicals and Reformers" and read the session plan. This session is somewhat different in that it covers four different faith groups (Mennonite, Amish, Quakers, and Brethren). Small groups are assigned to read articles about these groups and then think of a creative way to present their report to the class. You may want to round up a few art supplies (markers, construction paper, glue, newsprint or posterboard), as well as a grab bag of possible props for skits. A snack of Amish treats is optional. If you have access to books about or by the Amish, an Amish quilt, prints of paintings by Edward Hicks, Shaker music, or other items representative of any of these faith groups, bring them along and let the kids get a look at the culture of these groups.
Extending the Session	**1. Special Days** If your group is meeting in the Christmas season, arrange to attend a service of lessons and carols at a local Episcopal Church or bring in a recorded performance to capture some of the flavor of Anglican worship. If your group is meeting in Lent, attend an Ash Wednesday service. If your study falls around October 4, find out if any of the local Episcopal churches are doing a service of blessing of the animals on the feast day of Saint Francis of Assisi. **2. Canadian History** The Episcopal Church was the established church of Canada for many years of its history. Your class may be interested in exploring that history. They may want to examine more closely what it means to "establish" a religion and discuss the relationship between church and state. **3. How to Visit an Episcopal Church** This delightful article by Episcopalian George Harrison is found on page 4 of the newspaper. It's fun to read even if your group doesn't visit an Episcopal service. If you're planning a visit, the article will be very helpful and reassuring! Note that your teens may participate in the Eucharist if they've been baptized. Ask your group to be especially aware of how the service appeals to all of the senses and the whole person. See "How to Visit Another Christian Church" on page 12 for additional tips and suggestions. Asking an Episcopalian to visit your class is another option (contact the pastor of a neighboring church for suggestions on who to ask). See "Hosting a Guest from Another Christian Tradition" on page 11 for general suggestions and procedures.

72

If Group Members Are Adults or Young Adults

Step 1: People of all ages like to work puzzles, so don't hesitate to use this way to help them "take notes" on the article. Not convinced? See the nonpuzzle option to step 2.

Step 2: You may want to include some further questions about religious "bridges." Ask questions like these:

- **What other kinds of faith bridges are you aware of?**
- **How successful are these bridges at creating a place where two different traditions or faiths can meet?**
- **Why do you think the Episcopal Church succeeded?**

Another topic that adults may want to discuss is the role Episcopalians have played in the political heritage of our countries. Ask questions along these lines:

- **Why do you think that so many (more than any other denomination) United States presidents have been Episcopalian?**
- **How has the Episcopal Church shaped Canadian politics and society?**
- **In what ways and in what places does the church still act as a base of authority in contemporary society?**

Step 3: Here are some additional questions you may want to ask:

- **What "method" would a Reformed Christian use to ascertain an answer to a faith-related question?**
- **How do our sources of authority compare?**
- **What other similarities and differences do you note? How significant are they?**

Step 4: Don't underestimate the value of actually experiencing some of the Episcopal ways of worship described in the session plan. If members of your group have attended Episcopal worship services, ask them to lead this step and add their own reflections on why it was meaningful worship for them.

Step 5: The "flavor of worship" activity and questions should work well with adults and young adults. As leader, you may also want to take a look at the book *Authentic Worship in a Changing Culture* (available from Faith Alive Christian Resources: www.faithaliveresources.org or 1-800-333-8300) and use some of the discussion questions in this book to extend this part of the session:

- **Should worship embrace the "church of all times and in all places"?**
- **How can worship avoid becoming too limited to the here and now?**
- **If worship is narrative, what story does it tell? How is the story told?**
- **Should it be possible for Christians to "feel at home" worshiping with any Christian community, even one very different from our own? Why? If so, to what extent?**

The bidding prayer should be an excellent way to close the session.

Radicals and Reformers

6

Scripture/Confession	Romans 12:2; Heidelberg Catechism, Q&A 111

Session Focus

The Anabaptist and Quaker traditions originated out of radical attempts to reform the Christian church. The key faith distinctive of the Anabaptist tradition is an emphasis on keeping the world at a distance in order to live as a follower of Christ.

Session Goals

- to understand the reasons for the radical reformation
- to describe four kinds of radical Christian groups in this tradition
- to appreciate the role this tradition plays in holding up New Testament ethics
- to distinguish what it is to be "in and not of the world"
- to reflect on our own relationship to the world

Key Distinctive of This Faith Tradition

In the mid-eighties my family lived in eastern Pennsylvania and made frequent trips to Lancaster County, home to many Amish and Mennonites. At first I was a voyeur. I stared, wondered, and was amused by their definitive lifestyle. A friend who lived in Lancaster and worked with several Mennonites provided us with front-row seats for viewing this active community. He took us to their grocery stores and the used furniture stores the tourists didn't know about. We bought eggs from Yoders and had a quilt made by Anna Stolfutz.

As we got to know these people at a more personal level, I discovered that I was less amused and more challenged by their way of life. If my flavor of Christianity asked me to give up my college degrees, my charge cards, and my frequent flyer miles, could I? Would my faith be more meaningful if it cost me more to practice it? It might be easier, I decided. If the lines are clearly drawn and the boundaries between plain and fancy are firmly in place, it might actually be simpler to make ethical decisions, to know how to love a neighbor, to practice spiritual disciplines like prayer and fasting.

The Anabaptist faith tradition can be perceived as an "otherworldly" kind of Christianity, reflecting its interpretation of the biblical command to be *in* but not *of* the world. Anabaptists believe that Christians must keep the world at a distance in order to live as followers of Christ. To some extent, then, a Christian is defined by what he or she is *not*—not a soldier, not a follower of cultural dictates, not a citizen of any kingdom but God's. A Christian does not seek wealth, does not value his or her own interests over the interests of the church, does not assume a privileged position.

Reformed Christians are profoundly "this-worldly." We believe our world was lovingly and graciously created good by a God who continues to sustain and watch over it. We celebrate the gift of this world. God honored creation by becoming one of us; the Creator became the creature to redeem a world that had gone bad. We believe that salvation is holistic—an all-encompassing redemption that renews every square inch of the world and will restore creation to the goodness God intended it to embody. Because we can see through this world as it is to the way God intends it to be, we know we are called to work toward making that intended world a reality.

The Reformed tradition defines a Christian by what he or she *is*—a healer, a bringer of good news, an agent of redemptive change. A Christian does justice, loves deeply, walks humbly. A Christian seeks the welfare of others, works for the quality of life of all, and values the place in the world where God has asked him or her to live out that mission.

Materials	**Leader**

Leader
- Bible
- Participant newspaper: Radicals and Reformers
- Listing of local churches in these traditions from newspaper, yellow pages, or Internet
- 4 notecards, each with one of the following words: Quaker, Amish, Mennonite, and Brethren
- Creative supplies for group presentations: posterboard, newsprint, markers, colored construction paper, glue/tape, props for skits
- Instructions for small groups (p. 82), four copies
- Optional: Amish-made snacks (see suggestions in step 2)

Key websites you may want to check for more information:
www.mennonites.org
www.mennonitechurch.ca
www.quaker.org
www.brethren.org
www.thirdway.com

Participants
- Bible
- Participant newspaper: Radicals and Reformers

Note: This time we'll omit the Christian family tree; we'll return to it at the beginning of next week's session.

Session at a Glance

Step 1: We list three modern inventions we would miss if they were suddenly off-limits to us (5 minutes).

Step 2: We divide into four small groups, each reading about one faith group (Mennonites, Amish, Quakers, Brethren). Each group thinks of a creative way to present basic information about that faith group to the rest of the class (25-30 minutes).

Step 3: We present our reports to the rest of the class (20 minutes).

Step 4: We explore the relationship of Christians to the world, referring to Romans 12:2 (10 minutes).

Note: We suggest a minimum of an hour for these sessions. You'll find that you can easily expand that time, even adding an extra session on each faith tradition, using the unread articles in the newspaper and the ideas in the course introduction. If you must cut the time to, say, forty-five minutes, you'll need to omit some of the activities we suggest and shorten others. **In this session, for example, you could omit step 1, cut back on the number of faith groups studied in steps 2 and 3, and cut back on the number of questions you ask in step 4.**

Step 1

Getting Started

This session is a bit different from previous ones. You'll be dividing into four small groups that will spend the most of the session preparing and presenting their account of the radical group they have been assigned. Your role in this session is to be a facilitator and resource person.

If your class is small, it's OK to have groups of one. Two is better, of course. And three or more is ideal. See also the "small class" option to step 2.

To get started, distribute notecards and ask each person to list three twentieth-century inventions he or she would miss the most if, for some reason, they were suddenly declared off-limits and could no longer be used. Review responses, then bridge to the faith groups we are studying today. One of those does, in fact, declare a number of modern inventions such as electricity and automobiles to be off-limits. Take care not to suggest that all groups in this faith tradition take this stance; in fact, only the Amish consistently do.

Option: What's in a Name?

Instead of the above activity, try this. Before the group meets, locate a baby-naming book and look up the names of each member of your group (don't forget to include your own name). Type these meanings up as a handout and distribute to the group. Give them five minutes or so to individually guess which name means what, and then let the group find out whose name matches each meaning. You'll get some laughter about how our names don't always reflect our personalities or interests. Explain that today we'll be asking about the meaning of names given to various groups within this faith tradition: the Amish, the Brethren, the Mennonites, and the Quakers.

Step 2

Working in Small Groups

Divide the class into four groups of equal size ranging from one to four persons each. Having only one or two persons in a group will obviously limit the kind of presentation that's made (no skits!), but the format will still work.

Distribute one notecard and a copy of the small group instructions (p. 82) to each group. For your convenience, instructions are repeated below:

> In your groups, read through the article "The Third Way" (p. 1). Then read the article about the faith group your group was assigned (Mennonite, Amish, Quaker, or Brethren). You have twenty-five minutes to read the two articles and prepare a presentation on your faith tradition for the rest of the class. Your presentation can be anything you wish: an interview of a teen from this faith group, an impromptu skit, a talk show format, a sitcom, an interpretive poster, a game, new words to an old song—any way you can think of to answer the questions below. Try to make it interesting and fun!
>
> • What is the meaning of the group's name?
> • Where did it start? Why? How did it become part of Christianity in North America?
> • What does it believe?
> • How are its members expected to live?
> • What can this faith tradition teach other Christians?

Have some supplies available for groups to use: posterboard, newsprint, markers, construction paper, glue/tape, and, if you wish, a grab bag of props for skits.

While groups are working, circulate and offer help as needed. If you happen to live near an Amish community, consider distributing some Amish-made jam or apple butter or cheese on crackers. Corn (for popping) is another Amish treat available from roadside stands and in bulk food stores in Amish areas.

Option: For Small Classes

To put more kids in a group, cut back on the number of faith groups you cover. For example, choose only the Amish and the Mennonites instead of all four faith groups. Choose the ones the class is most interested in or that are most prevalent in your area.

Of course, you could also decide to simply read the articles together and then use the five bulleted questions for discussion.

Step 3

Presentations

Give the groups a five-minute warning and then reassemble for the presentations. Have the Mennonite group give their presentation *before* the Amish group—otherwise sequence doesn't matter.

After each presentation, allow some time for questions. If you think that any of the five bulleted questions (above) still haven't been answered, take time to discuss them further.

Option: Summary Questions

If time permits and you think the group could use a summary of the session so far, ask questions like these:

- **What do you think it means to be a peace church?**

- **According to these churches, what lifestyle choices does the New Testament teach Christians to make?**

- **If these churches are the "third way," what are the first and second ways?**

Step 4

Wrap-up

Have everyone stand up, form a circle, and place their left arm on the right shoulder of the person on their left. Tell them to move as far away as they can from this person and still maintain touch. Who has the longest reach?

Ask questions like these:

- **What do we mean when we say that we're keeping something at arm's length?** (Maintaining a certain level of distance.)

- **Why do we do that?**

- **What do these churches keep at arm's length?** (Government regulation, modern innovations, cultural expectations, war, wealth, consumer-driven values.)

Then have the group turn to Romans 12:2: "Do not be conformed any longer to the pattern of this world, but be transformed by the renewing of your mind.

Then you will be able to test and approve what God's will is—his good, pleasing, and perfect will."

- **How do these churches live out these words from Paul?** (They distance themselves from the world by keeping themselves separate from it. But you should note that these churches—especially the Mennonites—are among the most generous in helping the needy.)

- **What does it mean to be a nonconformist?** (To resist being like everyone else.)

- **If you are a Christian, do you have to be a nonconformist? Why or why not?** (Christians must be nonconformists when it comes to evil and destructive behavior—and that isn't easy, because sin can be terribly attractive. But we are also conformists. We conform to God's will for our lives, which always demands that we work at transforming evil to good.)

- **How do Reformed Christians differ from these Christians on relating to the world?** (Rather than retreating from the world and its evils, we believe God calls us to work within the world to fight injustice and other evils.)

- **Where do you find yourself in relation to the world? What potential dangers do you see?** (You may want to talk with the group about the trap of getting so caught up in the things of the world that people can no longer tell if we're Christians or not. We need to be *in* the world but not *of* the world.)

Close with one of the following prayers:

- Let your group reflect once more on their own relationship to the world, then pray silently to God, perhaps asking for forgiveness for letting the world have too much influence on their lives; or asking for help in not conforming to the world but in conforming to God's will for their lives. Open and close the prayer yourself.

- Use answer 111 of the Heidelberg Catechism. Say a line, then have the group repeat it in unison after you:

  Help us to do whatever we can for our neighbor's good.
  Help us to treat them as we would like them to treat us.
  Help us to work faithfully so that we may share with those in need.
  Amen.

- Use these lines from *Our World Belongs to God: A Contemporary Testimony,* stanza 6. Again, say the line, then have the group repeat it in unison after you:

  We rejoice in the goodness of God,
  renounce the works of darkness,
  and dedicate ourselves to holy living.
  As covenant partners,
  called to faithful obedience,
  and set free for joyful praise,
  we offer our hearts and lives
  to do God's work in his world.

Looking Ahead to the Next Session	Review the newspaper "The Baptist Tradition" and read the session plan. Decide which articles in the paper and which steps in the session you'll use with your group. Note any questions you have or any further reading you will want to do.

For step 5 of next week's session, you'll need to decide whether to explore the topic of infant baptism versus believer's baptism or take the option about different perspectives on the end times. |
| **Extending the Session** | **1. Simple Gifts**
Find and bring in some art that has been created by any of these four groups: for example, the paintings of Edward Hicks, Amish quilts, Shaker music or furnishings. Visit your library and bring in some books about these faith groups. Display the items and give the kids a chance to talk about them and how they reflect the culture and gifts of the group from which they came.

The peace churches are well known in the Christian community for their work in Third World countries. One of the ways they do that is through craft stores that provide a market for goods produced by people in high-need areas of our world. Locate a Ten Thousand Villages or SERVV store in your area, and ask if they can bring in a sample of the crafts that they offer for purchase.

If a CROP walk is being done in your area, consider participating as a group to raise money for world hunger.

2. Peacemaking
You may wish to discuss a topic this session doesn't address, but one that is a key distinctive of this tradition—peacemaking. Matthew 5 is the key Scripture text for this position. Just wars, taking life in order to serve a greater good, refusing to join the military, and nonresistance to violence are some of the issues that are part of the topic. For a Mennonite perspective on the issue, read John Howard Yoder's article "The Way of Peace in a World at War" in *Exploring Ethics* (a publication of Christian Schools International, available through Faith Alive Christian Resources, www.FaithAliveResources.org or 1-800-333-8300). Or read Yoder's book *The Politics of Jesus*.

3. The Amish and the Media
Locate a recording of the song "Amish Paradise" by Weird Al Yankovic (someone in your group will have it or can download it for you) or play a video clip from the movie *King Pin*, about an Amish bowling star. (Preview them both before you decide to use either.) Raise the issue of how the Amish are perceived by popular culture. Ask questions like these:

- **Based on what you learned today, how accurate is the way the Amish are portrayed by popular culture?**

- **Why does our culture think the Amish are a source for laughs?**

- **Why do we lack respect for others whose lifestyles are different from our own?**

- **What other groups in society experience this same kind of ridicule?**

- **Is there any way Christians can counteract these attitudes?**

4. Field Trip, Videos
Find out if any of these groups or other Christian utopian societies have established communities in your area and arrange a field trip. Another possibility is to visit an Amish settlement near your area. |

TRAVARCA offers several videos, including one that features an inside look at the Amish, that could be of interest for the group.

<table>
<tr><td>

If Group Members Are Adults or Young Adults

</td><td>

Chances are good that some members of your group have encountered the Amish in their various settlements. If so, encourage them to talk about their impressions of this group. Others may have experience with the Mennonites or the Brethren churches. Or perhaps someone has visited a Quaker service. Be mindful of the rich experiences your group brings to these sessions.

Step 1: If you're leading a class of older adults, you could ask them to mention three "modern" inventions they think are more trouble than they're worth, things they wouldn't mind living without, at least for a while. If you're using the option, you may want to ask your group members how they got their names or how they named their children. Perhaps they have some stories to tell about how they have dealt with an odd name.

Steps 2-3: Why not try the group work suggested for teens? Adults' presentations may lean toward the academic rather than the absurd, but urge them to be creative. Perhaps they can stage an Oprah-type talk show.

Step 4: You may want to include discussion on other topics in addition to or in place of the discussion about being in and not of the world. Here are some alternatives:

- Look at "Extending the Session" for suggestions on the topics of peacekeeping and our culture's attitude toward unique groups.

- The initial years of the Anabaptist movement were ones of persecution and extermination. You might want to look up and add the story of the siege of Munster. Which ideas of the Anabaptists might be supported by your church today? Which of their ideas would result in discipline if a member of your church advocated them? Are there fewer differences today between the Anabaptists and Reformed Christians? Why do you think so?

- In 1554, Menno Simons responded to an attack by a Dutch Reformed pastor named Gellius Faber, who called the Anabaptists conspirators, a devilish sect, and a false church. Part of Simons' response was the following list of the characteristics of a true church.

  1. The true church holds to the Word of God as its only standard for belief and practice.
  2. The true church practices baptism and communion the way the first Christians did.
  3. The true church shows love for its neighbors.
  4. The true church expects persecution—the "pressing cross of Christ."
  5. The true church boldly confesses Christ "in the face of cruelty, tyranny, fire, and the sword."
  6. The true church brings forth the fruits of Christ.

What does your group think of this list? What's missing? What's on it that shouldn't be? How does your denomination or congregation reflect these statements? Compare this description to Article 29 of the Belgic Confession. The "false church" mentioned in the article is the Roman Catholic Church, not the Anabaptists. How well do these two documents match each other? Would Simons disagree with the Belgic Confession's statement? Why is it important to be able to recognize the true church?

</td></tr>
</table>

Instructions for Small Groups

In your groups, read through the article "The Third Way" (p. 1). Then read the article about the faith group your group was assigned (Mennonite, Amish, Quaker, or Brethren). You have twenty-five minutes to read the two articles and prepare a presentation on your faith tradition for the rest of the class. Your presentation can be anything you wish: an interview of a teen from this faith group, an impromptu skit, a talk show format, a sitcom, an interpretive poster, a game, new words to an old song—any way you can think of to answer the questions below. Try to make it interesting and fun!

- What is the meaning of the group's name?
- Where did it start? Why? How did it become part of Christianity in North America?
- What does it believe?
- How are its members expected to live?
- What can this faith tradition teach other Christians?

The Baptist Tradition

7

Scripture/Confession	Genesis 17:7; Matthew 28:19-20; Acts 2: 38-39; Ephesians 1:4-5; Heidelberg Catechism, Q&A 70, 74
Session Focus	Churches in the Baptist tradition include a wide range of theology and worship practices; however, five common convictions unite them: the supreme authority of the Bible, believer's baptism, local church autonomy, evangelistic preaching, and separation of church and state.
Session Goals	• to understand that Baptists can differ theologically but still hold common convictions of faith • to identify the five key distinctives of the Baptist tradition • to distinguish between the theology of believer's baptism and infant baptism and to reflect on our own baptism (or to distinguish between Baptist and Reformed views of the end times) • to give thanks for one way in which this tradition can help our faith grow
Key Distinctive of This Faith Tradition	Baptist historians disagree about the origins of the Baptist tradition. Some say that the followers of John the Baptist passed on the legacy of baptism for the forgiveness of sins from his death until this day, and that Baptist churches are the current home of this distinctive New Testament call to salvation. We are Baptists, they say, because we are direct followers of John the Baptist. That's a gratifying idea, but it's hardly accurate. The modern Baptist churches of North America originated from a group of English Christians. Unhappy with the state of the Church of England, these people fled to the Netherlands, and there they encountered Mennonites. They embraced the idea that the new churches of the Reformation needed to model themselves after the New Testament churches. Worship, they said, should reflect the worship of that church—simple and spontaneous. Leadership should be charismatic, governance should be simple and local, and sacraments should be celebrated as recorded in Scripture. Today's Baptist churches still follow those directives: little liturgy, gift-based leadership, congregational church government, and baptism by immersion. For those of us who aren't very familiar with the Baptist churches, the variety among them can be dizzying. An American Baptist church can be as Reformed in doctrine and worship as any in our tradition, while a premillennialist fundamentalist church would strike us as radically different from anything in our experience. Appreciating the wide continuum in this tradition is the key to understanding why there are so many Baptist churches. All of them believe that their version of church is the most biblical, the most true to New Testament norms. Those kinds of exclusive claims have made it easy for congregations to leave one convention to form another, and to declare independence from all others who aren't as faithful to the truth as they are. If there is one part of the Baptist tradition that distinguishes it from all other Christian traditions, especially our own Reformed tradition, it would be the

high value placed on a personal experience of salvation and believer's baptism. For many of us who have never known anything but the contemporary evangelical language of being "born again," it may be hard to remember that our tradition places a high value on covenant relationship. We baptize infants because in baptism God's precious promises are signed and sealed to us well before we are even able to seek God out. Only later when we make public profession of our faith do we acknowledge to other believers that we have accepted these promises.

In the Reformed tradition, salvation is seen as a process, not a one-time event. It is a total commitment of heart, mind, and soul, not simply "asking Jesus into my heart." All of our life, not just our spiritual life, is to be lived under the rule of Christ. Salvation takes place in the context of the fellowship of other believers, not just "Jesus and me."

God reaches out to us in love before we are capable of even knowing who God is. Infant baptism publicly demonstrates that we are claimed as God's own long before we can even know that we have such an amazing parent. Help your group grasp that these two views of baptism are much more than proof text wars over infant versus believer baptism; they are two different ways of understanding how God works in our lives.

Materials	**Leader**
	• Bible
	• Participant newspaper: The Baptist Tradition
	• Newsprint, marker
	• Listings of local Baptist churches from newspaper, yellow pages, or Internet
	• Roll of masking tape
	• Optional: ten sheets of paper, each with one of the following words written in large print: general, particular, new light, old light, northern, southern, primitive, innovative, black, white
	• Optional: large poster of Christian family tree (see session 1)

Key websites you may want to check for more information:
www.sbcnet.org. (Southern Baptist Convention)
www.abc-usa.org (American Baptist Churches)

Participants
• Bible
• Participant newspaper: The Baptist Tradition
• Copy of Christian family tree (see session 1)

Session at a Glance

Step 1: We fill in the Christian family tree with the names of the Anabaptist groups from last week's session and with the Baptist tradition (5 minutes).

Step 2: We respond to ten belief statements, then discover that all ten describe the Baptist tradition (10 minutes).

Step 3: We read the article "What's a Baptist Church?" (p. 1) and note the many distinctions that exist between Baptist groups (10 minutes).

Step 4: We review the five beliefs typical of all Baptists, contrasting them with the Reformed tradition (15 minutes).

Step 5: We look more closely at baptism as practiced in the Baptist tradition and the Reformed tradition (10-15 minutes). An option is to look at differing perspectives on the end times.

Step 6: We give thanks for one insight or teaching of the Baptist tradition that can help our own faith grow (5 minutes).

Note: We suggest a minimum of an hour for these sessions. You'll find that you can easily expand that time, even adding an extra session on each faith tradition, using the unread articles in the newspaper and the ideas in the course introduction. If you must cut the time to, say, forty-five minutes, you'll need to omit some of the activities we suggest and shorten others. **In this session, for example, you could omit step 2 and shorten the number of questions you ask in steps 3 and 4.**

Step 1

Getting Started

Distribute copies of the Christian family tree to your group members. If you've made a large family tree poster, use it as a model to show the group where the various names should be written (or let them use the family tree diagram on p. 2 of the newspaper).

Have everyone write in "Anabaptist" on that branch, then mark the two smaller branches off that tradition: Mennonite and Brethren. Add the Amish as a splinter group off the Mennonite branch. Finally, add the Quaker branch, a splinter group coming from the Church of England. You may want to take a moment to quickly review what the names of these groups mean, along with some of the things they have in common.

Point out the part of the tree we'll be looking at today (the Baptist tradition). Help group members trace how it grows out of the Church of England, connects to the Mennonites, and then grows its own branch.

Ask the group why they think the branch is drawn this way. What can they guess about its history? Who do they think this group was? Have them write in the name Baptist.

Step 2

Yes, No, Not Sure?

Prior to today's session, use masking tape to mark three areas on your floor where the group can stand. Using masking tape or sheets of paper, print yes on one of the areas, no on another, and a question mark on the third. If masking tape on the floor doesn't work, put the same three signs on three separate areas of your classroom wall.

Have the group stand and move to their answer spot to respond to each statement you read aloud. Pause after each to give the group time to move.

1. **A Christian must be born again.**
2. **A Christian must have a personal relationship with Jesus Christ.**
3. **Baptism is a sign that you are saved.**
4. **Every word in the Bible is true.**
5. **Living a moral Christian life means I don't smoke, drink alcohol, listen to rock music, or watch R-rated movies.**
6. **God created the world in six twenty-four–hour days.**

7. **The church and state should be completely separate from each other.**
8. **God saves people through a different way today than the way that God saved people in the time of Moses.**
9. **Christ's second coming will involve a rapture of believers into the air and a time of tribulation or suffering for those left behind.**
10. **Evangelism is the job of every Christian.**

Note which of the ten was most rejected by the group and which was most acceptable. Ask for reasons behind the decisions on these particular statements. Comment that *all* the statements reflect the beliefs of the single largest Protestant group in North America: the Baptists.

Step 3

What's a Baptist Church?

If you haven't already done so, hand out the newspaper for today's session. Have volunteers take turns reading "What's a Baptist Church?" on page 1. Stop after each of the sections and ask the group to define the key distinctions:

- general/particular
- new light/old light
- northern/southern
- primitive/innovative
- black/white

Next, turn to "Facts and Figures" and read the introductory paragraph. Then have the kids note that a couple of these terms (general, primitive, southern) appear in the titles of the various Baptist denominations and groups that are listed in this article.

Option: Name Game

If you have time, here's an additional activity that demonstrates the diversity of Baptist churches. Distribute the ten sheets of paper you've prepared, each one with a name, as follows: *general, particular, new light, old light, northern, southern, primitive, innovative, black, white.* If your class is small, give some students two sheets. Explain that as you call off names, students are to stand in a row and display the names that you called. Call off five names in any order you wish (use only half of any given pairing of names). Here's an example:

1. General New Light Southern Innovative White Baptist Church

When the kids are lined up, ask them what this church believes, based on the descriptive words in its title. Try it with a couple more, as time permits (many combinations are possible!).

2. Particular Old Light Northern Primitive White Baptist Church

3. General Old Light Southern Innovative Black Baptist Church

After the group has sat down, explain that the first example is a true description of the Southern Baptist Convention. Ask them what they think is the point of the activity. Although they may come up with several responses, confirm that one point is to demonstrate the diversity of the many Baptist denominations. Have the group look at "Facts and Figures" again and point out where these words appear in the names of these churches. Do the same with your local Baptist Church listings.

Step 4

What This Church Believes

Explain that despite all these differences, all Baptist churches hold five principles central in their teaching. Walk through "What This Church Believes" (p. 3), pausing after each section to ask questions along these lines:

Authority of the Bible
- **Does the Reformed tradition also believe this?** (Yes. We too believe that the Bible is the only infallible authority for faith and life. Point out that fundamentalists—see definition in "Sound Bites" and article "Fundamentalism: What Really Matters"—take this a bit further and hold that the Bible is completely error-free. They also read the Bible very literally—for example, creation happened in six twenty-four–hour days. Be sure to point out that not all Baptists are fundamentalists, though many are.)

- **What impact do you think this belief about the Bible would have on Baptist worship services?** (Preaching and testifying are important.)

Believer's Baptism
- **How do Baptist Christians differ from Reformed Christians on this point?** (It's enough at this point to simply say that Reformed Christians believe that infants of believers ought to be baptized. Baptist Christians insist that a person must be old enough to accept Jesus as Savior and Lord before he or she may be baptized. You may choose to go into more detail on this in step 5 of the session. If you plan on using the option to step 5, you should take time now to talk about what believer's baptism versus infant baptism means as far as our approach to salvation is concerned—see "Key Distinctive of This Faith Tradition.")

Priesthood of All Believers
- **What implications does being considered a priest have in practical terms for your life?** (You can approach God directly instead of through a saint or a priest. You—along with other believers—can read and interpret the Bible for yourself. Like a priest, you can serve God and help others.)

- **What's the difference in the way Baptist Christians and Reformed Christians regard church structures and administration?** (Baptists give local congregations more power and autonomy than Reformed churches do. In addition, Baptists view church membership as a "voluntary association" that one chooses to make. Reformed folks see church membership in an organic way—we are born into the church as we are born into membership in a family or citizenship in a state.)

Preaching the Gospel
- **What is the "Great Commission?"** (Have someone read Matthew 28:19-20.)

- **What would you expect the Baptist churches to be very good at doing?** (Missionary work—bringing the good news of the gospel. Give due credit to the Baptists for having a great tradition of sharing the gospel with others.)

- **Who's the Baptist preacher who has preached to more persons than anyone else in history?** (Billy Graham—point out the article on page 4 for students to check out later.)

- **Why are Baptists so eager to tell the good news?** (Because Christ tells them to! And because they believe people need to make a decision for Jesus. Take a moment to note that the Reformed tradition also honors the Great Commission, though Reformed folks believe that people cannot respond to the gospel call unless God first gives them faith to respond; salvation is first of all God's decision, not ours.)

Separation of Church and State
- **Where do you think the Baptists got their idea of keeping church and state entirely separate?** (Baptist Christians come, in part, from Anabaptist roots—remember the Amish and Mennonites from the last session?)

- **Does that mean that Baptists have nothing to do with politics or government?** (No. Many Baptists, like many Reformed people, are active in politics and in working for the government.)

Summarize, saying something like this: **The unique feature of the Baptist tradition that sets it apart from all other Christian traditions, especially the Reformed tradition, is the high value it places on a personal experience of salvation and on believer's baptism.**

Option: Worship: Preaching and Testifying

It will only take a couple of minutes to read this short article. Doing so will quickly introduce participants to the wide range of worship activities in this tradition. Follow up by asking participants if they see anything different in a Baptist service that they might appreciate seeing in their own worship services.

Option: Return to Yes/No Questions

You may want to give your group a chance to ask questions about any of the ten statements (given in step 2) that we haven't yet "covered" in the session. In the earlier exercise, they were asked to decide **Do we believe this as Reformed Christians?** Ask if they would like to return to any of the statements for further discussion.

Step 5 ### More on Baptism (or the End Times)

At this point in the session, you can decide to explore in more detail baptism, a teaching that touches a deep difference in the way Baptists and Reformed folks regard the process of salvation. Or you can take the option at the end of this step and go in the direction of another key distinctive of most Baptist groups: their view on the end times. You may want to ask your group which topic they'd like to discuss.

 If you choose the topic of baptism, first have the kids draw some comparisons between our tradition and the Baptist tradition:

- When
  Baptist: after acceptance of salvation
  Reformed: in infancy (if born into a Christian family) or after public profession of faith (if a recent covert who was not baptized earlier)

- To whom
  Baptist: to believers only
  Reformed: to the infant children of believers or to older believers

- How
  Baptist: by immersion
  Reformed: by sprinkling

- Meaning
  Baptist: a profession of accepting Jesus as my Savior
  Reformed: God claims this person as a covenant child

- Status
  Baptist: my declaration of faith in Jesus
  Reformed: God's declaration that I belong to him

Note: You don't need to list these but do be sure the group is aware of these distinctions.

Share with the group that while sometimes we can get into arguing Scripture passages with Baptists about who's right and who's wrong on the infant/believer's baptism issue, the real difference between these two views isn't just about who is interpreting specific Scripture texts correctly. The real issue is what we think the Bible teaches about how God's grace is worked out in our lives. To make this clear, ask questions like this:

- **Who takes the first step in infant baptism? The person or God?** (God, because the baby can't. Have someone read Genesis 17:7 and talk about how God first reached out to us, establishing a covenant with us and promising to be our God. Our baptism is a reminder of this promise of God to always be our God. It is a sign and seal that we belong to God.
  Circumcision OT, baptism NT
- **Who takes the first step in believer's baptism? The person or God?** (The individual decides to believe.)

- **Which do you think offers more comfort and hope? How important to you is the knowledge that God loved you before you ever knew God? What does that tell you about God?** (You may want to read Ephesians 1:4-5: "God chose us in him before the foundation of the world, to be holy and blameless in his sight.")

- **What exactly does God promise us when we are baptized?** (To always be our God; that we are God's children; that our sins are forgiven in Christ if we receive those promises in faith—Acts 2:38-39.)

- **If you have been baptized, what does your baptism mean to you today? If you haven't been baptized, what do you think it would mean for you to be baptized now?** (This is the kind of question that invites a thoughtful, written response. If you have time, distribute notecards and give the group five minutes to journal their thoughts. Invite those who want to share their responses to do so.)

- **In baptism God says, "You are my child." What are we saying when we make a profession of faith or confirmation?** (We reply, "You are my God.")

Encourage those who have not yet done so to consider making that statement before God and the congregation.

If your group has access to a copy of the Heidelberg Catechism, you could ask someone to read Q&A 79 and 74 as a summary of this section.

Option: Uh, What Time Zone Are We In?

You may want to choose this option instead of the discussion about baptism in the regular step. Another possibility is to spend an extra session on it. See "Session Extensions."

Begin by asking a provocative question: **How many of you think that Jesus Christ will return before the end of your lifetime?** Ask for a show of hands and solicit some rationale for the responses made by group members. Acknowledge that "end times" is a topic that many Christians think a lot about, especially during times when events in our world seem to be spinning out of control. Explain that most Baptists have a unique view of what's going to happen before and after Jesus returns.

Take turns reading "Uh, What Time Zone Are We In?" (p. 4). There's a good deal of information compressed into this article, so allow time for it to "sink in" and for student questions. It may be helpful to put two timetables on your board or on a sheet of newsprint (we'll add some Scripture passages that you can refer to if you want to get into the details). This information comes from the leader's guide of "What We Believe," sessions 20-21, available from Faith Alive Christian Resources.

Premillennial
- *Trumpet and rapture.* A loud trumpet will announce the return of Christ; believers, dead and alive, will rise from the earth to meet him in the air (1 Thess. 4:13-18).

- *The tribulation.* A seven-year period of worldwide war and destruction, during which a worldwide government called "the beast" will take over. The Antichrist will dominate the world during this time. Some 144,000 Jews will be converted and will work to evangelize an evil world. All Christians will escape this terrible time in an event called the rapture (Matt. 24:4-8, 22).

- *The millennium.* After seven years of tribulation, Jesus will return and everyone will see him (Matt. 24:30-31). Satan will be locked in a pit (Rev. 20:1-3), and Christ's thousand-year glorious reign from the city of Jerusalem will begin (Rev. 20:4).

- *Satan briefly unleashed but destroyed.* Toward the end of the thousand years, Satan will emerge from the pit and make war against Jesus and his followers (Rev. 20:7-10). After a final battle, Satan will be cast into the bottomless pit and remain there forever.

- *Final judgment.* All unbelievers will be raised from the dead (believers have already been raised) and God will judge everyone (Rev. 20:11-13). Those who lived godless lives will go to hell forever; those who believed and ruled with Christ during the millennium will live forever in the new earth.

Amillennial or Reformed View

- *Christ returns.* Trumpet will announce it (1 Thess. 4:16). Everyone on earth will see him coming.

- *Dead raised first.* Then those who are still alive on the earth will be instantly changed to immortal beings and will meet Christ in the air (1 Thess. 4:16-17).

- *New heaven and earth.* God will burn this old world (2 Pet. 3:10) and the earth will then be renewed, refreshed, made new (2 Pet. 3:13; Rev. 21:1).

- *Final judgment.* Christ will judge the living and the dead (Rev. 20:12). Those who rejected Jesus will be punished eternally (Rev. 20:15), but those who love Jesus will live with him forever in the beautiful new earth (Rev. 21:1-3).

Ask the following questions:

- **What are the main differences between the two views?** (Note that the Reformed view includes only one return of Christ, not a "secret" return to remove all believers from the earth, then a public return to launch the millennium. The Reformed view does not include a rapture, and it does not take literally the one thousand years, the tribulation, or the leashing and unleashing of Satan.)

- **Does how we believe on this issue affect our salvation?** (No. And when we talk with Baptist Christians about the rapture or the tribulation or the thousand-year reign of Christ, it's good to keep in mind that we are discussing non-salvation issues with fellow Christians.)

- **Don't these things matter?** (Yes, they do, because they have to do with how we read and understand God's Word. So it's important to discuss our differences. But whether we believe in two distinct returns of Christ or one doesn't affect our salvation in Jesus Christ. As one Reformed pastor put it, "If someday I find myself floating in the air with Jesus, I'm going to smile at my Baptist friends and gladly say, 'Guess what? You were right!'")

- **What are some of your thoughts and feelings about the end times and Jesus' return?**

| Step 6 | **Wrap-up** |

Ask the group to think of one thing the Baptist tradition has to teach us—something that can help our own faith grow. For example, having a close, personal relationship with Jesus or boldly sharing our faith with others. Invite them to incorporate their idea into a sentence prayer of thanks to God for this faith tradition.

If focused on baptism in the previous step, you may want to close with this beautiful prayer from the sacrament of baptism in the Presbyterian Church (USA):

Merciful God, you call us by name
and promise to each of us your constant love.
Watch over your children, [name each member of your group].
Deepen their understanding of the gospel;
strengthen their commitment to follow the way of Christ;
and keep them in the faith and communion of your church.
Increase their compassion for others;
send them into the world in witness to your love;
and bring them to the fullness of your peace and glory;
through Jesus Christ our Lord,
Amen.

—from *Book of Common Worship*, page 416. © 1993, Westminster John Knox Press. Used by permission.

As group members leave, encourage them to read the rest of the newspaper at home and to save all the issues of the newspapers for their own future reference.

Looking Ahead to the Next Session

Review the newspaper on the Methodist tradition and read the session plan. Decide which articles in the paper and which steps in the session you'll use with your group. Note any questions you have or further reading you wish to do.

Prior to next week's session, we suggest you prepare four "quote" posters or sheets to display in your classroom (see step 3). And you'll need to provide copies of a hymn by Methodist songwriters John Wesley or Fanny Crosby.

Extending the Session

1. End Times Option
Taking a close look at the end times could make an exciting topic for an additional session. See the option under step 5. You could also check to see if your church or a neighboring church has the video course *What We Believe*. Get the last (of four) video segment of the course, and try session 20 ("End Times: Premillennialism") and session 21 ("End Times: The Reformed View"). In these videos of about 20 minutes each, Pastor Lew Vander Meer clearly spells out how these views differ in a way that your high schoolers will find interesting and memorable. You could also rent the videos from TRAVARCA (see p. 13). The leader's guide for sessions 20 and 21 will give you lots of good ideas for additional discussion.

2. Fundamentalism: What Really Matters
Read this article on page 3, if you haven't already done so in your regular session. Then, with more advanced groups that are interested in this topic, discuss the distinctive way Reformed Christians understand Scripture as opposed to the fundamentalist way. Explain the words *inerrant* and *infallible* and talk about the variety of ways Christians use these words. Direct them to a passage such as 1 Corinthians 11:3-16 and have them interpret the passage as if they were fundamentalist and as if they were Reformed.

Here are some discussion questions you may want to use:

• **What is the primary meaning of the passage?**

• **If you were a fundamentalist and applied Scripture literally, what would this passage mean for the women and men in your church?**

- **How would a Reformed Christian approach this passage?** (Consider its context, that is, what it meant to its original recipients and how it would be comparable today; ascertain the principle behind the instruction.)

- **When the Bible doesn't quite match the context of our current culture, what do we do? Ignore the Bible? Change the culture to fit the Bible? How do we decide which is the correct thing to do?**

3. Attempt Great Things for God

The modern missionary movement was the inspiration of a Baptist minister and was spearheaded by the Judsons. Explain this to your group, then spend some time reflecting on missions, missionaries, and the Great Commission. If someone in your congregation or in your group has mission experience, have them share these experiences. But be sure to talk about how we can also be witnesses for Jesus Christ in our day-to-day lives. Which speaks louder: our actions or our words? How can we witness to our friends without losing their friendship?

As part of your discussion of evangelism, you could also show a video about Billy Graham (see TRAVARCA listings on p. 15). Let the group get a sense of how Graham captured the hearts of North Americans as he became as our "national pastor."

4. Civil Rights Movement

Read the article "Hall of Faith: Martin Luther King, Jr." (p. 2) and use it to discuss King and the civil rights movement. **Would the civil rights movement have succeeded without the involvement of Black churches? Why or why not? How did Christian principles and ideals influence the movement?** You may also want to show a TRAVARCA video on Martin Luther King, Jr.

5. Reminders: Field Trip, Guest Speaker, Video

If there's a Baptist church in your area whose worship services are sufficiently different from your own, consider planning a visit. See "How to Visit Another Christian Church" on page 12 for some helpful tips and suggestions. Ask your group to be especially watchful for how the service emphasizes some of the five Baptist distinctives taught in this session.

Check out the half-dozen videos that TRAVARCA has to offer on the Baptist tradition (see p. 15 for details and ordering information).

If Group Members Are Adults or Young Adults

Here are some additional suggestions for your older group.

Step 1: Be sure to take a moment to ask group members about any previous experience with and first-hand knowledge of the Baptist tradition. Someone with a great deal of knowledge in the tradition can even take over as leader for part or all of the session.

Step 2: You can use the questions as a hand-raising survey instead of moving around the room.

Step 3: Have the group determine which two combinations of the descriptives would be furthest apart. Which combination would be the closest to the Reformed tradition?

Step 4: As suggested in the option, you can add the article "Worship: Preaching and Testifying" to this step. Draw on the experiences of those in your group who have visited Baptist services.

Step 5: Talk with your group about what baptism means to them as parents. How does baptism join their parenting to God's? Was baptism a significant moment in their faith journey? Why? Further discussion could also focus on the "proof texts" that Baptists use to refute infant baptism. How important is this issue?

If you decide to take a longer look at millennialism, you may want to consult the November 5, 2001, issue of *The Banner* and in particular Wayne Brouwer's article "Moving on After Left Behind" (call the *Banner* office for a photocopy of this article—1-800-333-8300). Brouwer suggests asking these four questions about how we see the future:

1. Does God unfold the plans of salvation for humankind in basically two large and related segments (Israel and the church—each experiencing a variation on the same covenant theme) or in seven smaller and relatively distinct ways (as Dispensationalism reads the Bible and history)?

2. Is there a rapture of the church?

3. How should we interpret the "thousand years" of Revelation 20:2-7?

4. Is there likely to be a "purgatory"?

See the article for fuller discussion. You could also show a video clip from the movie *Left Behind* or have someone who has read the books share a review of them with the group.

For a thorough and very readable discussion of the Reformed perspective on the last days, try reading Andrew Kuyvenhoven's *The Day of Christ's Return: What the Bible Teaches, What You Need to Know* (available from Faith Alive Christian Resources, www.FaithAliveResources.org or 1-800-333-8300). See especially chapters 4-7.

The Methodist Tradition

8

Scripture/Confession	Ephesians 1:3-6; Romans 8:28-39; Heidelberg Catechism, Q&A 61
Session Focus	The value of personal piety demonstrated through prayer, Bible study, good works, and lifestyle choices has distinguished this faith tradition and influenced North American cultural standards of Christian behavior.
Session Goals	• to understand how Methodism began as a movement to revitalize the private faith of Christians, not to reform a tradition or in reaction to false teaching • to describe the Methodist Quadrangle • to appreciate the many ways this faith tradition has influenced North American cultural standards of Christian behavior • to reflect on one thing we learned from this faith tradition that could help strengthen our own faith
Key Distinctive of This Faith Tradition	In the eighteenth century, Western Europe was a place of growing tensions: an agrarian society was becoming industrial, the Age of Reason was replacing an age of faith, and established churches were increasingly unable to address the philosophical and social demands these changes were making on issues of faith and life. The result was a broadening thirst for a more personal faith and resistance to allowing authoritarian structures of church and state to govern choices of belief. Pietism was the name given to this movement. Under its banner, Christians spoke out for personal Bible study, renewal of the priesthood of all believers, authentic practice of faith, more practical training of ministers, renewed concern for nonbelievers, and the application of teaching and preaching to daily life. Meeting in small groups in homes or barns and gathering for joint worship in fields, these Pietists grew rapidly into independent churches. Rediscovering Reformation principles, they applied them to the context of their times, creating what was called "true religion." What was this true religion? Anchored in the study of Scripture, it called for personal experience of God and required that faith be practiced in daily life through the spiritual disciplines of prayer, Bible study, good works, and lifestyle choices. In effect this movement re-created Protestantism. In the Netherlands this Pietistic movement broke away from the state Reformed church to form a new church (which was the mother church of the Christian Reformed Church). Through the influence of the Moravians of Germany, it led two brothers, Anglican ministers, to moments of illumination that changed their lives and created a new Christian faith tradition. This new faith tradition, called Methodism, defines modern evangelical Protestantism. The Reformed/Presbyterian tradition has adopted and been influenced by this movement—in same cases, leading to new denominations. Whether influenced by continental Pietism, revivals in Scotland, or the Great Awakening of

the New World, who we are as a tradition today has been further refined by its key values. How then does our tradition still differ from the Methodist tradition that was fully formed by this movement?

The key difference lies in theology. Reformed theology interpreted the study of Scripture, practice of spiritual disciplines, and personal knowledge of God through the lens of God's sovereignty and role in salvation. Thus the Reformed tradition maintained a strong hold on election, predestination, and sanctification. In contrast, the Wesley brothers embraced an Arminian theology, which held that people can choose to accept or reject the gospel, that no one is chosen to be saved, and that it is possible through spiritual discipline to arrive at a place where sanctification is complete.

As your group studies and discusses the Methodist faith tradition, you'll want to celebrate its role in revitalizing a stagnant faith, in bringing the Bible back to the common people, in inspiring worship with new songs of praise, and in helping us see that faith is lived out in our lives, not just in our minds. You'll also want to help them see that, while embracing all of these, we can still acknowledge the wonder of God's choosing of us, finding us, and bestowing on us the gift of salvation.

Materials

Leader
- Bible
- Participant newspaper: The Methodist Tradition
- Newsprint, marker
- Listings of local Methodist churches from newspaper, yellow pages, or Internet
- Four quotes from step 3 written out as posters and hung in your room
- Your denominational hymnal or a copy of a hymn by Charles Wesley or Fanny Crosby (see step 5 for titles; optional: an overhead transparency of this hymn and markers)
- Optional: large poster of Christian family tree (see session 1)

Key websites you may want to check for more information:
www.uccan.org (United Church of Canada)
www.umc.org (United Methodist Church)
www.amecnet.org (African Methodist Episcopal—AME)

Participants
- Bible
- Participant newspaper: The Methodist Tradition
- Copy of Christian family tree (see session 1)
- Notecards

Session at a Glance

Step 1: With a partner, we invent a club and "sell" it to the group. The leader tries to sell the idea of the "holy club" founded by John and Charles Wesley (15 minutes).

Step 2: Working with a partner, we read the history article "Committed to a Method" and sample aspects of Methodism that surprise us and aspects we appreciate (15 minutes).

Step 3: We read "What This Church Believes," look for ideas that support four key quotes, then discuss and summarize them (10 minutes).

Step 4: Using up to five short articles, we add to our list of things to appreciate about the Methodist tradition (10-15 minutes).

Step 5: We wrap up the session by exploring how a Methodist hymn reflects the faith of that tradition (5 minutes).

Note: We suggest a minimum of an hour for these sessions. You'll find that you can easily expand that time, even adding an extra session on each faith tradition, using the unread articles in the newspaper and the ideas in the course introduction. If you must cut the time to, say, forty-five minutes, you'll need to omit some of the activities we suggest and shorten others. **In this session, for example, you could use the timesaving options provided for steps 1, 4, and 5.**

Step 1

Getting Started

Tell the group that today they get to create a club—not a weapon but a group! They will have complete freedom of choice in deciding the purpose of the club and what it does, but each club should have the following (list these on a sheet of newsprint):

- Name
- Rules for membership
- Leader(s)
- Benefits—why would someone want to join your club?

Have kids work in groups of two or three so to create clubs, so you'll have at least a couple of clubs. Give them about five minutes to create their club, then have them try to "sell" it to the rest of the class. If you've got plenty of time today, you could distribute poster paper and let them make an ad for their club.

Conclude by trying to sell the "holy club" to your group (you may want to make a poster advertising its features).

Here is the information you'll need to describe your club:

- *Name:* The Holy Club
- *Rules for membership:* One hour of daily prayer first thing every morning; meet with the other members of the club for two hours of Bible study and reflection every evening; no card playing, gambling, use of alcohol, or profane language.
- *Leadership:* My brother and I are the only leaders.
- *Benefits:* Support for living a Christian life, a deeper relationship with God, better knowledge of the Bible, opportunity to witness to others by your lifestyle.

Anyone want to join your club?

Explain that two college students named John and Charles Wesley actually created the "holy club." From it was born the Methodist denomination, which is the second largest Protestant faith group in North America today.

Distribute the Christian family trees and have everyone complete the Methodist branch, which emerges out of the Church of England (see p. 2 of the newspaper for placement of the Methodist branch).

If you're using the large family tree poster, have someone write in the Methodist branch.

Option: Timesaver

Have group members pair off and give each pair a sheet of paper. Allow two minutes for them to name as many student organizations or school clubs they can think of. See which pair has the most listings and share a few samples from a couple of lists. Bridge to the idea of a "holy club" as described in step 1.

Step 2

Committed to a Method

Distribute the newspaper for this session and have the group turn to the article "Committed to a Method" (p. 1). Partners (from step 1) can read the article aloud to each other (or silently, if they prefer). Each pair should jot answers to the following questions on a notecard:

- What are two aspects of the Methodist story that surprised you?
- What are two things you appreciate about this tradition?

After ten minutes, have the groups read their notecards aloud. Point out that it comes as a surprise to many people that the huge Methodist denomination came from two brothers who merely wanted to deepen the spiritual life of those who were already members of the Church of England. They had no intention of reforming that church or of beginning their own denomination.

Focus especially on the "appreciation" factor, jotting down ideas on newsprint as students mention them. Here are a few possibilities you might want to raise if the students don't mention them:

- emphasis on practicing the faith
- simple piety
- joy in being a Christian
- informal worship
- ethnically inclusive
- advocates for social justice
- an emphasis on unity, reconciliation, forgiveness

Quickly review "Facts and Figures" and include your local listings. Ask the group what in its history would support the fact that the Methodist Church is the most ethnically diverse Protestant denomination (not much, according to what we read). Lead to the next section by commenting that perhaps the reasons for its diversity has to do with its beliefs rather than with its history.

Option: Variation

For a change of pace in a larger class, have each pair try to find another pair with one or more similar answers to the two questions above. This will get kids milling around and reading each other's responses. See who can get the most matches or near matches in five minutes. Let groups report what matches or near matches they found.

What This Church Believes

Write the following quotes from this article on single sheets of paper and hang them in your room prior to the session:

- "I'd rather be a Methodist, with a round and shining face, than to be a long-faced Calvinist, that damns near half the race." (from an eighteenth-century song)

- "Undoubtedly faith is the work of God and yet it is the duty of man to believe." (John Wesley)

- "Christian faith is revealed in Scripture, illumined by tradition, brought to life in personal experience and confirmed by reason." (*United Methodist Book of Discipline*)

- "As to all opinions which do not strike at the root of Christianity, we think and let think." (John Wesley)

Point out the signs with the quotes and have a volunteer read them aloud. Then ask everyone to read (silently) the article "What This Church Believes." As they read, they should underline key sentences in the section that help explain the quotation. When everyone is finished, have the group check their answers with each other (or quickly review answers with the whole group).

For further discussion, ask some of the following questions:

- **What's the difference between the Methodist view and the Reformed view on the role we play in our own salvation?** (Methodists emphasize human choice—we choose to turn to God; Reformed/Presbyterian churches emphasize God's role—God chooses us, we do not choose God. You may want the group to read Ephesians 1:3-6 and Romans 8:28-29, both of which support the Reformed belief of God choosing us. See also Q&A 61 of the Heidelberg Catechism.)

- **Do you think we have the ability to turn toward God on our own? Do you think it makes a difference what you believe about how redemption happens?**

Scripture
Reason
Tradition

- **What's the difference between the Methodist Quadrangle and the Episcopal three-legged stool?** (Methodists add the idea of personal experience.) **Do you think the four points of the Quadrangle are a useful way to approach issues? Why or why not?**

- **How would personal experience affect the way we read a parable like, say, the parable of the prodigal son?** (Methodists say that personal experience brings Scripture to life. If we, like the prodigal, have let our sin separate us from the love of the Father, the parable takes on deeper and richer meaning for us).

- **Do you think it's possible that two Christians can read the same Bible text, come to different opinions about what it means, and both be right? Explain.**

- **Methodists have emphasized "holy living" more than other denominations. What do you think are the benefits or drawbacks of this?** *Legalism?*
Attention focused on actions, behaviors
Acknowledgement of importance of actions.

Re-ask the question about diversity in this tradition:

- **What in Methodist theology would support its ethnic diversity?**
  (The permission to be different).

Summarize the discussion so far by listing the key theological Methodist principles the group has discussed:

- The unconditional love of God.
- Christ died for all.
- Human beings may freely choose to accept or reject salvation.
- Grace is more important to know about God than judgment.
- Issues are to be decided by the quadrangle of the Bible, tradition, experience, and reason.
- Christian living is more important than Christian thinking.

Step 4

Additional Articles

Assign these five articles to pairs or to individuals, depending on the size of your group (either have kids keep the same partners as in steps 1 and 2 or form new pairs):

- "Worship: Shouting Methodists" (p. 3)
- "Riding in Circles" (p. 3)
- "Do All the Good You Can" (p. 4, up to "WCTU")
- "WCTU" and "Social Principles" (p. 4)

Allow about five minutes for reading the articles. Then call attention to the list of things to appreciate about the Methodist tradition that your group developed in step 2. Ask if there's anything we could add to the list, based on the articles we just read. Are any of the items on the list supported by these articles?

Lists will vary according to what the individuals who read the articles find to appreciate. Here are a few ideas you may want to add or emphasize:

- simple, easy-to-follow, informal worship services
- variety of songs
- a time of prayer with the congregation kneeling together
- commitment to evangelism
- strong concern for social justice
- concern for the environment
- desire to fight racism, poverty, and so on

Option: Timesaver

If your group is small and you're running low on time, read and discuss only the article on worship and the article on social principles. Have volunteers read the articles aloud, then add to the list of things to appreciate, as in the regular step.

Step 5

Wrap-up

Select a Charles Wesley or Fanny Crosby hymn from your denominational hymnal (consult the index of authors). Some examples:

- "And Can It Be"
- "Oh, for a Thousand Tongues to Sing"
- "Rejoice, the Lord Is King"
- "Blessed Assurance, Jesus Is Mine"

If it's Advent season, try "Come, Thou Long-Expected Jesus" or "Hark! The Herald Angels Sing." For Easter, choose "Christ the Lord Is Risen Today."

Distribute copies of your hymnals (or a photocopy of the hymn you chose) and read through the stanzas. Explain that the words to the songs we sing in worship reflect what we believe. Ask questions like these:

- **What phrases, if any, reflect Methodist beliefs or distinctives?**

- **What does the fact that this song is in a Reformed/Presbyterian hymnal tell you?**

- **Do you think we are more like or unlike the Methodists? Why?**

- **What's one idea from this tradition that you can use to help your own faith grow?** (Allow a minute for everyone to reflect, then invite responses, including your own.)

Close by saying the Wesleyan Covenant on page 4 of the newspaper in unison:

> I am no longer my own, but thine.
> Put me to what thou wilt, rank me with whom thou wilt.
> Put me to doing, put me to suffering.
> Let me be employed by thee or laid aside for thee,
> Exalted for thee or brought low by thee.
> Let me be full, let me be empty.
> Let me have all things, let me have nothing.
> I freely and heartily yield all things to thy pleasure and disposal.
> And now, O glorious and blessed God, Father, Son, and Holy Spirit,
> Thou art mine, and I am thine.
> So be it. Amen.

Option: Timesaver
Omit the hymns and use only the last bulleted question above. Have kids write their ideas on notecards and give the unsigned cards to you to read aloud.

Option: Overhead
Make an overhead copy of the hymn and project it. Use markers in two different colors to mark phrases typical of the Methodist and of the Reformed traditions.

Looking Ahead to the Next Session

Review the newspaper "The Holiness and Pentecostal Traditions" and read the session plan. Decide which articles in the paper and which steps in the session you'll use with your group. Note any questions you have or further reading you will want to do.

You'll need three cans of similar-looking colas (see step 1).

You might also want to think about showing a clip depicting Pentecostal worship from the movie *The Apostle*. (This is strictly optional, however.)

Extending the Session

1. *Extemporare* Prayer
Note the brief reference to this practice in the worship article. Explain that this kind of prayer involves everyone kneeling, then praying aloud as the Spirit moves them. There are no guidelines or organization to the prayer. Ask your group if they are willing to try this.

Set a minimum time limit of five minutes for the prayers, explaining that even if no one says anything, we will be on our knees in prayer during this time.

Afterward, evaluate this as a way to worship and pray together. Would it work with our congregation?

2. United We Stand
Methodists have been on the forefront of the ecumenical movement, calling denominations to unite under the things they share as Christian churches.

Show your group the church page from your local newspaper. Ask them to imagine that all these churches would be united into one. What advantages would they see? What disadvantages?

Carry this further, if time permits, by having kids work in small groups to some basic articles of belief that all these churches could support. Have them write these statements on newsprint, and then critique the statements with the entire group.

Return to the advantages/disadvantages question and see if students have anything to add to their earlier thoughts.

3. Social Principles
Get a full copy of the Social Principles of the United Methodist Church (available on the website) and discuss it carefully with the group. Where do they agree? Disagree?

4. Reminders: Field Trip, Guest Speaker, Video
If you're going to visit a Methodist Church, we suggest you check to see if there are any AME (African Methodist Episcopal) churches in your area. Check their website for locations (amecnet.org). See "How to Visit Another Christian Church" on page 12 for some helpful tips and suggestions. Ask your group to be especially watchful for how the service incorporates some of things they appreciated (see step 2) about the Methodist tradition.

Asking a Methodist to visit your class is another option (contact the pastor of a neighboring church for suggestions on who to ask). See "Hosting a Guest from Another Christian Tradition" on page 11 for general suggestions and procedures.

TRAVARCA has a video on Methodist camp meetings that your group might find interesting.

If Group Members Are Adults or Young Adults

Step 1: Instead of the "creating a club" activity, adults could talk about organizations or clubs or small groups that have been or are a meaningful part of their lives.

Step 2: Extend the discussion with the groups' experiences and firsthand encounters with Methodist churches. Give adults the choice of working alone or working in pairs. You may also discuss the role Pietism has played in our own denominational histories. Do a bit of reading, if necessary, so you can offer some specific details on how your denomination was influenced by the Pietist movement (Christian Reformed Church leaders could see *Our Family Album* by James Schaap, available from Faith Alive Christian Resources). Also, see the appendix of *Reformed: What It Means, Why It Matters* for a brief discussion of the Pietistic mindset within the Christian Reformed Church. Discuss, using question like these:

- **Which key characteristics of Pietism are still true today in Protestantism?**
- **Which have changed?**
- **Do the world and the church need a new movement like Pietism in order to meet the challenges our postmodern world presents to our faith life and practice?**

Step 3: Here are a couple of additional topics you could choose to cover:

- Assign the group a familiar passage such as the parable of the prodigal son or Psalm 23. Have them interpret the passage using Methodist quad as described in the participant newspaper.

- You may also want to talk further about grace and compare the Methodist understanding with that of the Catholic Church or the Lutheran Church.

- Explore the differences between the Arminian "free will" concept of salvation and the Calvinistic view of salvation. A good aid for you as a leader is chapter 7 of the leader's guide of *What We Believe* available from Faith Alive Christian Resources. Check out the video for this session as well—it's a good one to show to adults and young adults.

Step 4: Your group might enjoy singing a Charles Wesley or Fanny Crosby hymn.

The Holiness and Pentecostal Traditions

Scripture/Confession	1 Corinthians 12:1-11; Ephesians 4:4; 1 Peter 4:10-14; Heidelberg Catechism, Q&A 53
Session Focus	Arising out of the sanctification emphasis of Methodism, Holiness and Pentecostal churches emphasize the work of the Holy Spirit—Spirit baptism—in the life and faith of believers. These traditions emphasize an experience-based faith, not a text-based faith.
Session Goals	• to explain the relationship between Methodism and Holiness and Pentecostal churches • to describe the process of "entire sanctification" as taught by this tradition • to appreciate the desire to experience one's faith (a key distinctive of this faith tradition) • to identify the ways different traditions understand sanctification/holiness • to reflect on what this faith tradition teaches that can help strengthen our faith
Key Distinctive of This Faith Tradition	When I was a college student, the charismatic movement was in full swing in the Catholic Church. One semester, while taking a course on "Contemporary Faith Expressions," the class was assigned to attend and observe a charismatic prayer meeting at a local parish. Catholics speaking in tongues! What could be more strange than that? It was a long way from my psalm-singing Reformed roots. The evening disappointed. Our group of six students sat in a circle of folding chairs staring at each other, embarrassed, while all around us a high school gymnasium echoed with the voices of Christians in prayer huddles. We'd expected to see ecstatic utterances and hear uncontrollable speech. Instead we felt like intruders on a prayer meeting. That experience is typical of the attitude many of us share about this tradition. It looks pretty strange to those of us on the outside. We wonder what really goes on in worship. If the charismatic TV preachers are representative, it must get pretty wild, we think. Putting our hands on a television while Oral Roberts prays for healing is about as strange as it can get. Yet this tradition has given the broader Christian community a great gift: a new way of thinking about the importance of the person and work of the Holy Spirit. We have to admit that the Evangelical culture puts a lot of emphasis on the second person of the Trinity, and the Reformed tradition is pretty happy talking about the first. The Holy Spirit can seem somewhat nebulous and wispy—just who is the Holy Spirit anyway, and what's the job description? We like to talk about sanctification as a process that brings us more and more in step with our Savior, but who makes those steps possible? And who urges us to pray? Who comforts us in times of trial? Who never leaves our side? Perhaps Holiness talk isn't something we should dismiss so quickly. We need to ask how it can inform our sometimes-lean understanding of the Holy Spirit.

That aside, this tradition's emphasis on a second salvation experience does not square well with a Reformed understanding of Scripture. Ephesians 4:4 states quite clearly, "There is one body and one Spirit—just as you were called to one hope when you were called—one Lord, one faith, one baptism; one God and Father of all, who is over all and through all and in all." Our redemption is complete at the time we believe God's promise of salvation; our baptism is the only sign and seal we need to affirm our relationship to God.

Still, we have to admit that the notion of "entire sanctification" can be appealing. A dramatic "second conversion" experience (baptism of the Spirit), speaking in tongues as a sign of that baptism, and a heart that's totally cleansed from sin are powerful confirmations of faith. Maybe we can even envy a faith tradition that is so clear about the steps toward "entire sanctification."

In reality, the Christian life isn't nearly that straightforward; the signs of spiritual growth aren't always so clearly marked. And isn't that the way we prefer our journeys anyway? Lots of surprises, moments of joy, occasions of hope, and most of all, times when we don't know where we're going and need to rely on the guide who walks beside us, gently but urgently empowering us.

Materials

Leader
- Bible
- Participant newspaper: The Holiness and Pentecostal Traditions
- Newsprint, marker
- Listings of local Holiness and Pentecostal churches from newspaper, yellow pages, Internet
- Three clear plastic cups labeled 1, 2, or 3 for each participant
- Three different kinds of cola soft drinks
- Optional: large poster of Christian family tree (see session 1)

Key websites you may want to check for more information:
www.nazarene.org (Church of the Nazarene)
www.wesleyan.org (Wesleyan Church)

Participants
- Bible
- Participant newspaper: The Holiness and Pentecostal Traditions
- Copy of Christian family tree (see session 1)
- Notecards

Session at a Glance

Step 1: We do a fun experiment showing the importance of experience, a factor that the Holiness and Pentecostal faith traditions emphasize (5 minutes).

Step 2: We look at the history of the Holiness and Pentecostal traditions, noting that the driving quest behind both traditions is for "entire sanctification" (10 minutes).

Step 3: Using the article "What These Churches Believe," we look at the relationship between holiness, sanctification, and the Spirit (10 minutes).

Step 4: We place these traditions on the Christian family tree (5 minutes).

Step 5: We take a quick but appreciative look at worship in these traditions (10 minutes).

Step 6: We use Scripture to discuss "the gifts of the Spirit" and reflect on what these traditions offer that can help our own faith grow (15 minutes).

Note: We suggest a minimum of an hour for these sessions. You'll find that you can easily expand that time, even adding an extra session on each faith tradition, using the unread articles in the newspaper and the ideas in the course introduction. If you must cut the time to, say, forty-five minutes, you'll need to omit some of the activities we suggest and shorten others. **In this session, for example, you could omit step 1 (or take the option), omit step 5, and reduce the number of questions in step 6.**

Step 1

Getting Started

You'll need a set of three identical clear plastic cups for each group member and three different brands of cola drinks (Pepsi, Coke, Faygo or whatever brands you wish). Using a marker, write 1, 2, or 3 on each cup. Pour a small amount of one cola in cup 1, another kind in cup 2, and a third in cup 3. Be sure to make a note to remind yourself what brand of pop you poured in each cup!

When each person has a set of labeled and filled cups in front of him or her, ask, **Can anyone identify the different kinds of pop in these cups without tasting the pop?** Confirm that this can't be done.

Show the group the three bottles or cans from which you poured the pop (but do not link them with any of the cups). Ask, **Does it help if I tell you that the pop in the cups came from these three bottles (or cans)? Can you tell what brand is in each cup now, without actually tasting the pop?** Again, confirm that while the odds have dramatically improved, we still can't say with certainty what brand is in each cup.

Ask, **If the liquids look identical, how can you tell the difference?** Obviously, only by tasting. Invite group members to take a sip of each and to guess the kind of pop in cups 1, 2, and 3. Reveal what's in each cup. Reiterate that only by tasting did we have any kind of a chance of guessing what was in the cups.

Write these words on a sheet of newsprint or on your board:

- sanctification
- holiness
- Spirit-filled

Then ask the following questions.

- **Based only on prior knowledge, how would you define the words?** (Chances are you'll get descriptions, not definitions, and they'll be very similar. Point out how closely related these words are to each other.)

- **What would it take for someone to be able to define these words with real understanding?** (Experiencing them—first-hand knowledge.)

Introduce the Holiness and Pentecostal traditions by explaining that these traditions value religious experience over religious knowledge or belief.

107

Option: Timesaver

Ask the group what the following situations have in common:

- A coach who knows the game but has never played it.
- Someone who's read about fixing computers and is eager to remove your hard drive and fix it, but who has never taken a computer apart before.
- Saying that you hate lobster based only on observing them in a tank at your local store.
- Knowing Jesus by reading all about him.

For more fun, dramatize these for the kids, if you wish. Be the coach who knows the rules but hasn't played the game, the guy who's ready to take apart someone's computer, and so on. Better yet, have kids role-play these situations.

In each situation, of course, the missing factor is experience. Bridge to the faith traditions being studied today as traditions that value religious experience over religious knowledge or belief.

Step 2	**Searching for Sanctification**

Hand out the resource and direct your group to the lead article "Searching for Sanctification" and its sidebar "A Teen Describes 'Spirit Baptism.'" Have the group read it silently, circling three words—*holiness, sanctification,* and *Spirit*—every time they come across them in the reading.

When they're done, review the content with the following questions:

- **What tradition did these churches come from?** (Methodism.)

- **What was the driving quest behind these two new movements? What were they searching for?** (Complete sanctification, holiness, being Spirit-filled.)

- **What were the three waves of Pentecostalism in the twentieth century?**

Next to the three words on your sheet of newsprint (holiness, sanctification, Spirit) put up the number of times they occurred in this article. You'll be continuing this word count in the next step.

Step 3	**What These Churches Believe**

Direct the group to "What These Churches Believe" (p. 3). Also read the sidebar "Baptism in the Holy Ghost." Have group members take turns reading the article aloud to the group; again have the rest of the group keep track of the three words. Once again do a word count and add it to the numbers on the board for total sums. Which one is mentioned the most? Ask, **If *grace* was the key word for Lutherans and *sovereignty* for the Reformed, what is the key word for these traditions?** (Spirit.)

Read the definition of "entire sanctification" from "Sound Bites" on page 2. Then ask the following questions:

- **How are *sanctification, holiness,* and *Spirit* related, according to these traditions?** (A first or initial sanctification is followed by a second sanctification that results in a state of holiness. Being Spirit-filled is a sign either of that second sanctification, or, in some of these churches, a third and complete sanctification.)

- **How does a believer know where he or she is in the process?** (By what he or she has experienced.)

- **In what ways does this tradition stress the work of the Holy Spirit over the work of Jesus Christ?**

- **What's the good thing about that emphasis? What's not so good?**

Step back and make sure your group is still with you at this point. Ask if they have any questions about sanctification and all the many ways it is discussed in this tradition.

Then have students quickly scan "Sound Bites" (p. 2) and "What Does It Mean to Be Holy?" (p. 2). Use the articles as a summary of this step.

Step 4   Family Tree, Facts and Figures

Use the family tree to show how the Holiness churches come from the Methodist branch and the Pentecostals from them (see newspaper, p. 2). Your Christian family tree should now be complete! Check to see if anyone still needs to add information from other faith traditions to their copy of the family tree.

Take a quick look at "Facts and Figures" and your own local churches in this tradition. Note the statistics and the large and growing numbers of these churches. Ask, **Why is this such a popular and growing tradition?**

Go back to the opening sentence of the lead article and read it with the group again: **"Suppose the Entire Sanctification Pentecostal Foursquare Gospel Church of God recently bought a house on your street and renovated it as a place of worship."** Ask, **What does the name of this church mean?** Your group should be able to see now that these are four descriptives with specific meaning. Would this be a church they would like to join?

Step 5   Worship: Giving the Spirit Room

Take turns reading this brief article on page 3. You may want to supplement it by showing a clip from the movie *The Apostle.* Another possibility is to use this section to prepare for a visit to a holiness or Pentecostal congregation in your area.

Discuss the article by asking, **What do you find appealing about this kind of worship service? Why?**

You may also want to talk about worship customs from these traditions that have become part of the worship of some churches in the Reformed tradition (raised hands, praise songs, services of healing). This may well be the part of the session that intrigues your group the most, so be prepared to give them a little more time, as needed.

Wrap-up

Say something like this: **We've been talking about sanctification, holiness, and the work of the Spirit from this tradition's perspective. But how do we evaluate these ideas?**

Distribute Bibles and ask someone to read Ephesians 4:4 aloud. Ask, **What does this verse say about a second baptism of the Spirit?** (There is only one baptism, not two.)

[handwritten in margin: Rms 12:6]

[handwritten above Ephesians 4:4: +5]

Say, **What about the gifts of the Spirit? If a girl in your Bible study at school told you she was praying that you would be blessed with the gift of tongues and sanctification, what would your reaction be? What would you do if you attended youth group at her Assemblies of God church and someone in the group started speaking in tongues? Freak out? Hope it happens to you too? Should you pray that you could experience this gift of the Spirit? What does our church teach about this gift of the Spirit?**

Take turns reading 1 Corinthians 12:1-11 aloud. Ask questions like these:

- **Does the Holy Spirit give each person a gift?** (Yes.)

- **Are these gifts the same?** (No, there are different gifts; two of them are healing and speaking in tongues.)

Ask someone to read 1 Peter 4:10-11.

- **What does Peter say is the purpose of our gifts?** (To use them to serve God and others.)

- **How do we know what gifts we have from the Spirit?** (We see them working in our lives; someone tells us that we have that gift; we take a course like *Discover Your Gifts* and learn what they are.)

- **Are spiritual gifts a mark of the depth of our faith or the state of our sinlessness?** (No. They are simply gifts that the Spirit gives us to use for the good of the church.)

- **Can we experience sanctification without speaking in tongues?**

- **How can you know that the Holy Spirit is active in your life?**

You may want to read this quote from Robert DeMoor's *Quest of Faith* (Faith Alive Christian Resources):

> **Already in this life the Holy Spirit begins to purify us. He replaces our selfishness with the love of Christ. He replaces our despair with hope and our unbelief with true faith. He gives us gentleness, kindness, patience, and forgiveness. He makes us nail our old selves to Christ's cross and helps us walk in his footsteps. He makes us hate evil and love the good. One day he will remove completely our old nature and perfect the new. As the life-giver, he will remove all suffering, sin, and evil from us. He will fully make us what we already are in Christ: saints.**
>
> —Quest 22

Assure the group that if we have received salvation through faith in Jesus Christ, then the Holy Spirit is at work within us in the lifelong process of becoming more and more what God wants us to be—images of Christ.

If your group has access to the Heidelberg Catechism, you may want to read Q&A 53 together at this time.

- **What can you learn from the Holiness and Pentecostal traditions that could help your own faith to grow?** (Allow time for reflection, then invite those who wish to do so to share their thoughts with the group.)

For your closing prayer, use the words of a song that comes out of the Holiness or Pentecostal tradition, such as "Majesty" and "Precious Lord, Take My Hand."

Or use the words of the song "Spirit of the Living God." Follow with a time of silence. If you wish, invite group members to hold their hands up in front of them, palms up, in a gesture of receptivity and openness to the Holy Spirit.

Still another possibility is to offer sentence prayers directed to the Holy Spirit, giving thanks for the work of the Spirit in our lives.

Looking Ahead to the Next Session

Review the newspaper "Nondenominational Christianity" and read the session plan. Decide which articles in the paper and which steps in the session you'll use with your group. Consider taking an extra session to incorporate one or more of the many suggestions for extending the session.

To make the word cards for the word game in step 1, you will need all ten student newspapers for next time.

Extending the Session

1. Media Stuff
Videotape one of T. D. Jakes's sermons or talks and let the group capture some of the dynamic charisma of this Pentecostal leader. Or show all or part of the film *The Apostle,* starring Robert Duvall. Duvall based his role on actual Pentecostal and Holiness preachers, including T. D. Jakes.

2. Discover Your Gifts
Helping your teens discover their gifts can be a very affirming and enlightening experience for them. You might want to devote a session or even an entire course to this topic. A good resource is *Discover Your Gifts and Learn How to Use Them* (Youth Edition), available from Faith Alive Christian Resources. This action study introduces the concept of spiritual gifts and helps teens identify working gifts (gifts they're using now) and waiting gifts (gifts they are developing but haven't used yet). Includes a leader's guide and student book. Six sessions (but you could use only the gifts questionnaire and have only one extra session).

3. Visits, Guest
If there's an Assembly of God church in your area, arrange a visit for your group in the coming weeks. Prior to your visit, review the worship article with your group and check out the website of the church you're visiting so group members will have an idea of what to expect. Be sure to talk through the experience afterwards using questions like the following:

- **How would you describe this kind of worship?**
- **Was there anything that made you uncomfortable?**

- **Were there elements of this worship that you wish were part of our worship services?**
- **How different or similar was the service to that of your church?**
- **How is the Holy Spirit present in other kinds of worship?**
- **What makes worship acceptable to God?**

Another possibility is to invite a member of a Holiness or Pentecostal congregation to visit your class (contact the pastor of a neighboring church for suggestions on who to ask). See "Hosting a Guest from Another Christian Tradition" on page 11 for general suggestions and procedures. Perhaps your group would enjoy hearing a member of the Salvation Army explain the organization and its work.

If Group Members Are Adults or Young Adults	**Step 1:** If yours is a coffee-drinking bunch, try the opening activity with flavored coffees instead of pop.

Step 2: Your group might also like to discuss the various stages in the sanctification movement. Why would the Methodists have decided the movement was going "too far"?

Step 3: You can do a more thorough discussion of sanctification as this tradition defines it and as other Protestant traditions define it. You may also want to take a closer look at the "Foursquare" gospel. What distinctions do you think are being made? How does it compare to the Reformed teaching that Christ is prophet, priest, and king?

Step 5: Of course you will want to draw on the experiences of adults or young adults who have attending Holiness or Pentecostal worship services. And how about discussing the appeal of some Pentecostal preachers on television?

Step 6: Here are some suggestions for going deeper into evaluating various aspects of these faith traditions.

- Discuss the practice of speaking in tongues. You group might want to double check the New Testament reports of people speaking in tongues. Consult the adult version of *Discover your Gifts* (available from Faith Alive Christian Resources) for a comprehensive but succinct discussion of this gift.

- If members of your group are mature Christians, encourage them to share what the process of sanctification has meant to them. Do they feel "holier" now than when they were new Christians? What is the process of sanctification for them?

- Your group might also like to discuss the topic of faith healing. Compare what these traditions teach about healing to the Reformed position. What are the dangers in this kind of theology of healing and faith? Do we ever talk this way about perceived lack of answer to prayer? What can happen if someone prays to be healed and is not healed? Do you know someone who was healed this way? How did they describe their experience? Does God still heal through miraculous means like direct answer to prayer? An excellent resource is *Miraculous Healing and You: What the Bible Teaches, What You Need to Know,* by Henry Wildeboer (available from Faith Alive Christian Resources).

- Some of your members may have read one of Jim Cymbala's or T. D. Jakes's books. If so, have them share an opinion about the book in the light of what they have learned about this faith tradition.

112

Nondenominational Christianity

10

Scripture/Confessions	John 17:20-26; *Our World Belongs to God: A Contemporary Testimony,* stanza 44; Heidelberg Catechism, Q&A 54
Session Focus	Many of the churches of the twenty-first century resist denominational labels and maintain their independence as separate congregations. An increased emphasis on spirituality rather than beliefs fuels this move away from denominationalism.
Session Goals	• to understand how evangelicalism has taken a defining role in North American Christianity • to define *Christian* and *denomination* • to appreciate the possibilities open to North American Christianity as it begins the twenty-first century • to reflect on the contributions of the faith traditions we studied and how they can enrich our own faith
Key Distinctive of This Faith Tradition	That the status and place of Christianity is being challenged as our world enters a new century cannot be disputed. Increasingly we read and hear phrases like "the end of Christendom," "postmodernism," and "neo-evangelical." We are told that our role as spiritual leaders and authority setters in North American culture is no longer a given. In the years ahead, the church will need to deal with what may be a crisis in denominationalism. Corwin Smidt, who has studied Christianity and society for many years, cites the impact of a rising secularism and declining religious influence not just in our general culture but also within our own Christian traditions. Fewer people believe in a transcendent reality; more are inclined to see all religions as equally valid. Faith is becoming more about what we do in private and less about belonging to a named church or denomination. There is a growing sentiment among Christians that denominational labels have arisen from historical hurts that should have been healed long ago or from differences in cultural beginnings, rather than from substantial theological differences of opinion or credible distinctions of belief. What implications does this have for us as we conclude this study of the major Christian faith traditions and denominations of North America? The article "Church Now" in the student newspaper mentions some of these: growing diversity within denominations instead of between them, increased use of words like "evangelical" instead of "Baptist" in naming faith traditions, smaller denominational structures as emphasis shifts to local ministry rather than global outreach, and increasing loyalty to a specific congregation rather than a denomination. Are denominational distinctions a carryover from the past? Are we entering a century of an ever-increasing call to one North American Christian church?

113

Probably not. Denominations will continue to play a part in helping Christians define what they believe and think through their faith, as well as providing them with the resources they need to actively carry out their lives of discipleship. Named Christian traditions will still be the hallmark of congregations as they seek to give new and potential members a sense of continuity with the historic church of Jesus Christ and help them understand the "flavor" of the church they are joining.

Most significant for the survival of denominations will be the way they help congregations worship, nurture, and send their members out to do missions. That mission, which can never fail to excite the hearts of Christians, includes extending the kingdom of God to new horizons, expanding its borders in three dimensions, adding to the number of its citizens, and welcoming its King when he returns to claim it in all his royal glory.

Our future as a Reformed faith tradition lies in that joyful vision. "Hallelujah! For our Lord God Almighty reigns. Let us rejoice and be glad and give him glory! For the wedding of the Lamb has come, and his bride has made herself ready" (Rev. 19:6-7).

Materials	**Leader**
	• Bible
	• Participant newspaper: Nondenominational Christianity
	• Newsprint, marker
	• Complete set of participant newspapers
	• Notecards with "Soundbite" words from entire course written on them (see step 1)
	• Listing of local independent, nondenominational churches from newspaper, yellow pages, or Internet
	• Fish bowl or other large glass bowl and slips of paper
	• Handout: "The Mission of God's People" (p. 122, one photocopy per group member)

Key website you may want to check for more information:
www.Willowcreek.org (Willow Creek Church)

Participants
• Bible
• Participant newspaper: Nondenominational Christianity

Session at a Glance

Step 1: We play a word game to review some of the key words associated with each faith tradition we studied (15 minutes).

Step 2: We read "Church Now" (up to the "Church Next" section) and talk about what we would look for if we were "church shopping" (10-15 minutes).

Step 3: We write predictions for the church of the future, then compare our ideas with those found in the "Church Next" section of the main article (10 minutes).

Step 4: We read "So What Is a Denomination?" then discuss extremes to avoid and ideas/practices we've learned from other faith traditions that have the potential of helping our own faith grow (10-15 minutes).

Step 5: We play another quick round of the word game, then take a look at the mission of the one church of Jesus Christ throughout the world (10 minutes).

Note: We suggest a minimum of an hour for these sessions. You'll find that you can easily expand that time, even adding an extra session on each faith tradition, using the unread articles in the newspaper and the ideas in the course introduction. If you must cut the time to, say, forty-five minutes, you'll need to omit some of the activities we suggest and shorten others. **In this session, for example, you could omit step 1 and take the timesaving option for step 5.**

Step 1	## Getting Started

Begin with a word game that will help your group review the key ideas of the denominations we've studied. Go back through the newspapers and copy key words (not the definitions) from each newspaper's "Sound Bites" on notecards, one word to a card. On the top of the card write the category (faith tradition) that the word is related to. Shuffle the deck. Set up a pad of newsprint (on a stand) and supply markers (or use your board, if there's sufficient room to draw).

Divide your group into two teams and decide who goes first. The rules are quite simple:

- Taking alternate turns, each team gets a word card.
- One person on the team acts as the "artist"—he or she announces the category (Methodist, Roman Catholic, and so on), then sketches something on the newsprint that will help the rest of the team guess the word. You may want to supply the artist with a set of newspapers so that he or she can look up the definition and find some clues about what to draw.
- The "artist" position rotates every time a team takes a turn.
- No verbal or physical communication is allowed.
- There's a one-minute time limit to guess a word (use an egg timer or watch).
- A group can continue to draw and guess new words until the minute is up.

When you've gone through the deck the game is over. The team that guesses the most words is the winner. If you wish, consult the rules of the board game Pictionary for additional refinements you may want to add to the game.

Option: Variations

If your group enjoys role play or drama, make this a game of charades instead.

Here's a game you can play instead of Pictionary or charades. Ahead of time, write the key words in "Sound Bites" on notecards, one word to a card. Make a set of matching definition cards. Give half the cards and matching definition cards to one team. Give the other half of the words and definition cards to the other team. See which team can match up all their cards the quickest. Have the teams read their matches aloud.

Note: You can use the cards in other ways too. For example, you could give the word cards to half the class, and the definitions to the other half. Give them five minutes to mingle and find the matching cards. See what other variations you can think of!

M _____

P _____

B _____

w

group to name all nine faith traditions we've studied for far in
n ask questions like the following:

churches that don't belong to one of these traditions?
do you think some churches don't belong to any par-
nomination?

urch belong to a Christian tradition and not be part
nination in that tradition?** (Yes; in fact that's often the case
st and Pentecostal traditions.)

newspaper for today's session and take turns reading the lead
h Now." Read *up to* the section called "Church Next" (p. 2). After
uestions like the following:

5
V

- **Does it really matter what church you belong to? Why or why
  not?** (Kids will think you're expecting a yes here and may oblige with a
  muted response; tell them you're really interested in their opinions and
  encourage them to talk).

4

- **What kinds of questions would you ask if you were "church
  shopping"?** Jot down their responses on a sheet of newsprint or on your
  board. Their questions may focus on welcome and worship issues but nudge
  them to include theological questions as well. (Is the preaching biblical?)
  Once you have a short list, ask the following questions:

6

- **Would our own church pass this list?** (If your group has visited
  another church, ask how that church stacks up against the list.)

7

- **Under what circumstances would you shop for a church?** (Moving
  to a new place; don't like something that has happened in the current
  church.)

8

- **When, if ever, is it OK to leave your current church because you
  are unhappy there?**

9 DO SPECIFIC
DOCTRINES MATTER?

Conclude this section by reading through the definitions in "Sound Bites" on
page 2. Focus especially on the word *evangelical*. Notice that it can be applied
to any Protestant who believes in the divine inspiration of the Bible, personal
conversion to Christ, and the Great Commission. Note also that in the United
States, approximately 98 million Christians consider themselves evangelical.
Be sure students understand that this term cuts across denominational lines.

Option: Quiz

You can also include the quiz "Are You an Evangelical?" (p. 3) with this step.
After everyone has taken the quiz and added up their score, point out that all
the items on the quiz are beliefs of evangelicals.

Step 3

I Predict

Hand out strips of paper and show the group a glass fish bowl or other large
clear bowl. Ask them to play fortuneteller and write a prediction about the
church on their slip. How will Christianity or the church in North America
change in the next twenty years? You might want to give them an example

like the following to get them started: "I predict that black and white denominations in the same tradition will merge together as one church." Then have them fold the slips and place them in the bowl.

Now direct them to read the "Church Next" section of the main article "Church Now" (see p. 2). Ask them to underline the predictions made in the newspaper by the author of this course.

When everyone is done, list these on newsprint or on your board. Your list should include the following:

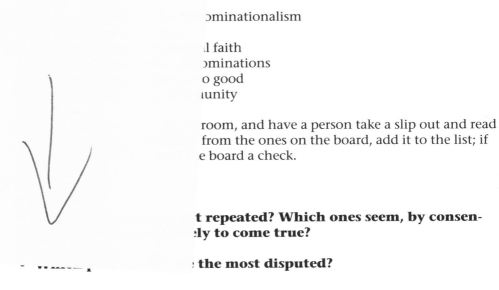

ominationalism

il faith
ominations
o good
unity

room, and have a person take a slip out and read
from the ones on the board, add it to the list; if
e board a check.

t repeated? Which ones seem, by consen-
ely to come true?

the most disputed?

<table>
<tr><td>Step 4</td><td>

So What Is a Denomination?

Have kids pair off and take turns reading "So What is a Denomination?" (p. 3) to each other. While they are reading, write the following questions on newsprint or on your board:

- **So what is a denomination?**
- **Why so many?**

Review the answers when they are finished reading. Point out that the word *denomination* isn't in the Bible. (Review the definition in "Sound Bites," p. 2.) You might also refer to "Facts and Figures" on page 1 to give the group a better sense of the major denominations in the United States and Canada.

Ask the group if they can think of two extremes to avoid when thinking about denominations. Listen to their suggestions. If they don't mention these extremes, do so yourself: first, to simply ignore our differences and pretend they don't matter; second, to think and act as if all other denominations are wrong and only your own is the true church.

Remind the group that we've studied nine major Christian faith traditions. Then ask questions like the following:

- **What is the value of knowing about Christian traditions and denominations that are different from your own?**

- **Do you think that the denominations we studied are more alike or more different from each other?**

</td></tr>
</table>

- **T_ ink back over the faith traditions we studied. What ideas or _ctices from one or more of these traditions could help you _ spiritually?** (Give kids time to reflect on this important question. _ with them one practice or idea from another tradition that could _ or strengthen your faith. Then ask for their comments.)

---

ion of the Church

_ that you are going to play one last round of the word game. Put _ back in their teams and tell them that no one may use the _ r diagrams of the previous team members. Call this the chal- _ e a stack of cards ready, but this time each card has the same _ ee how long it takes for your group to catch on to what's

_ ver, comment on the ways the group interpreted the _ _itions/visuals focus on the individual who is a _ any attempt to use a church to define it?

_sk some of the following questions:

- **What defines a church as Christian?** (It proclaims the gospel of Jesus Christ; practices the sacraments; grows, disciplines and encourages disciples; shows love; is a community of faith and fellowship; cares for the poor; speaks for those who are voiceless.)

Distribute photocopies of the handout "The Mission of God's People" (see p. 122). Have someone read this selection aloud (or read it in unison). Ask:

- **What does this testimony say the church is "about"?** (Being sent out. Point out that "mission" and "missile" come from the same root word—a missile is a weapon with a mission!)

- **What kind of missile is the church, according to the list in this paragraph?** (A missile of the gospel, discipleship, compassion, hope, forgiveness, new life.)

- **Is the mission of the church to grow the church (more members, bigger denominations, and so on) or to grow the kingdom of God?**

- **Do all the churches of Jesus Christ have this same mission?** (Yes, though some may emphasize different parts of it.)

- **What do you think will be the criteria that God uses to judge all denominations at the end of time?** (How well they fulfilled God's mission for the church.)

- **How do you see your church accomplishing this mission? How do you see yourself being deployed?**

Close by reading John 17:20-26. Then invite group members to offer sentence prayers of thanks or requests for the one, worldwide church of Jesus Christ, for all Christians everywhere.

WITH ALL THESE DIFF CAN WE WORK TOGETHER

WHICH DOCTRINES CRUCIAL?

Option: Timesaver

As a substitute for the above step, read John 17:20-26. Then hand out note-cards and ask everyone to write a brief statement saying what they believe about the one, worldwide church of Jesus Christ. Share responses, then conclude by reading in unison Q&A 54 of the Heidelberg Catechism as a confession of faith.

Extending the Session

1. More to Celebrate
Spend more time developing your group's appreciation for the gifts each of these faith traditions has contributed to Christianity. Divide into several small groups of two to four students each. Divide up the ten student newspapers (your copies) among the groups. Give each group a sheet of newsprint and ask them to come up with an expanded list of what they found to celebrate in each one. Post the lists on your board and review the lists together. In your closing prayer, have kids take turns giving thanks for one specific gift from each tradition.

2. What's Christian About Music?
What does your group think about Christian contemporary music? Read the article "What's Christian About Music?" and discuss the author's opinions. You could also bring in a recording of the Jars of Clay song "Hymn" and have your group listen to it while they read the lyrics in the resource. Talk together about what it means to make "faith-informed choices" when it comes to listening to music.

3. Survey: Teens Care About Religion
Check out the article by this title on page 3. Do your teens agree with George Barna that teens want "a church that makes God real, religion fun, provides them with a chance to find truths that are comprehensible and relevant, and does not strangle them with a list of don'ts"? Did anything about the survey surprise them? Disappoint them?

4. Parachurch
Read the article "Of Paracletes and Parachurches" (p. 2). Ask if any of your group have had experience with parachurch organizations such as Campus Life (you might bring a *Campus Life* magazine to show them), Young Life, Fellowship of Christian Athletes, or (for older groups) InterVarsity. Let them talk about their experiences and say how these organizations help their faith grow.

Consider inviting a representative from a parachurch organization to come to your group and describe what they do and how it helps churches and Christians.

5. More on Evangelicalism
You might like to focus a bit more on evangelicalism. Have the group review the definition in "Sound Bites" and take the quiz on page 3. Bring in a Veggie Tales video and have your group evaluate how it reflects evangelical themes.

6. Master Timeline
Divide into several small groups. Assign two or more faith traditions to each group and give them your copies of the newspaper for those faith traditions. Their task is to select an event from the timeline of their faith tradition that they think is most significant in the history of that faith tradition. Draw a line on an unrolled paper tablecloth (the kind used to cover tables at church functions). Have groups place their events on the timeline in chronological order, writing a brief caption for each event. Which of all nine events does your

119

group think is the most significant of all? If they could add another event to it sometime in the next hundred years, what would it be?

7. Visits and Videos
Visiting a nondenominational megachurch such as Willow Creek in the Chicago area could be a great experience for you and your group. Find one in your own area that would be fun for you and your group to visit.

If you can't make a field trip, try the TRAVARCA video *An Inside Look at the Willow Creek Seeker Service: Show Me the Way* (116 minutes). Recorded live, this video presents a Willow Creek Community Church seeker service in its entirety. Also features a dialogue with Bill Hybels, Nancy Beach, and Lee Strobel. See page 13 for ordering information.

If Group Members Are Adults or Young Adults

If some of your adults are newcomers to the faith who have joined your congregation precisely for some of the reasons given in the newspaper (they found a home in your congregation, not because of your denomination), you can have some excellent discussion on the issues raised in this session.

Step 1: Adults enjoy this game too. You might want to add some additional words from the resources to expand the vocabulary used.

Step 2: This discussion could get personal for your group since they may have had to "shop" for a church. Group members may be able to provide you with the real lists they've used to shop around for a church. Don't evaluate them, just affirm their items.

Step 3: Here are some additional questions to ask:

- **We know what the church has looked like for the past two thousand years and for the past two hundred and fifty years in North America. What can we learn from those past images to tell us what we'll look like a hundred years from now?**
- **What do you think would be a preferred future for the church? A worst-case scenario?**
- **What's the biggest challenge facing the church in this decade? The next twenty-five years? The next century?**
- **How does the diminishing importance of Christianity to our history and culture affect our present? Our future?**

Step 4: Here are some additional questions to explore:

- **Do you think that denominations are inevitable or a scandal?**
- **Do the issues that divided denominations in the past still divide them today or are there new differences?**
- **How do we decide that one denomination is right and others are wrong? Or is that an inaccurate way of naming the distinctions?**
- **How could the churches of the Reformed/Presbyterian tradition model more unity?**
- **As you reflect on the origins of your denomination, was a split necessary? Is reunification a possibility?**

Step 5: Extend the question of how each Christian tradition plays a unique role in carrying out the mission of the church. For example, how would you describe how Methodists have understood the mission of the church? Baptists? Consider going through each tradition and naming them.

Here are some additional areas for discussion

1. Ask your group how being a member of a denomination benefits your particular congregation. (This question may even come spontaneously from the group!)

Some possible answers to consider: gives a sense of identity and belonging; makes resources—like this one—available for study, worship, outreach, and spiritual growth; helps extend the congregation's witness through global ministries in partnership with other congregations regionally or nationally; provides mutual support and accountability for ministry through judicatories like a presbytery, classis, or synod; provides a system of Christian education that includes colleges and seminaries; offers a common confession that strengthens the congregation's witness. What others can your group name?

2. In the study questions for a book by Mark Noll called *Turning Points; Decisive Moments in the History of Christianity*, Robert H. Lackie gives the following four reasons for studying our Christian history:

- The study of the history of Christianity provides an ongoing reminder that the God of the church is not removed from life, but works out his will in the history of the world.

- The study of church history provides perspective on the interpretation of Scripture.

- The study of the church gives us fascinating glimpses into the ways Christians have interacted with their culture.

- The study of the church reveals again and again how God has mercifully protected and increased his church despite the sometimes horrendous abuses of those who call themselves Christians.

Share these four reasons with your group as a way to evaluate this study. How have they seen these four reasons unfolding in the stories of these ten different traditions of Christianity?

**The Mission of
God's People**

Following the apostles, the church is sent—
sent with the gospel of the kingdom
to make disciples of all nations,
to feed the hungry,
and to proclaim the assurance that in the name of Christ
there is forgiveness of sin and new life
for all who repent and believe—
to tell the news that our world belongs to God.
In a world estranged from God,
where millions face confusing choices,
this mission is central to our being,
for we announce the one name that saves.
We repent of leaving this work to a few,
we pray for brothers and sisters
who suffer for the faith,
and we rejoice that the Spirit
is waking us to see
our mission in God's world.

—Our World Belongs to God: A Contemporary Testimony, stanza 44